The Land and People of the
ARABIAN PENINSULA

Perhaps no land on earth is as much in people's minds and in the news as the oil-rich Arabian Peninsula. In recent years this desert region has soared in importance as its oil has become an indispensable source of energy to industrialized economies throughout the world. The changing life-style resulting from this oil wealth stands in dramatic contrast to the Arabs' traditional nomadic way of life as well as to the romantic images evoked by *The Arabian Nights.*

Much of what we know of Arabia does indeed err on the side of the romantic—the tales of Scheherazade describe sultans and harems and jewels, but tell nothing of the blazing sun that scorches a million square miles of sand, nor of the hardships and conflicts of life in a barren land. All that is behind the Arabs now. In this penetrating survey Mary Louise Clifford presents the eight nations of the Arabian Peninsula in a realistic light, describing the geography, religion, language, and political history that set this region apart, and depicting the cultural shock that results as nations and peoples struggle to adjust to the ultra-modern society swept in on a tide of oil.

PORTRAITS OF THE NATIONS SERIES

THE LAND AND PEOPLE OF AFGHANISTAN
THE LAND AND PEOPLE OF ALGERIA
THE LAND AND PEOPLE OF THE ARABIAN PENINSULA
THE LAND AND PEOPLE OF ARGENTINA
THE LAND AND PEOPLE OF AUSTRALIA
THE LAND AND PEOPLE OF AUSTRIA
THE LAND AND PEOPLE OF THE BALKANS
THE LAND AND PEOPLE OF BELGIUM
THE LAND AND PEOPLE OF BOLIVIA
THE LAND AND PEOPLE OF BRAZIL
THE LAND AND PEOPLE OF BURMA
THE LAND AND PEOPLE OF CAMBODIA
THE LAND AND PEOPLE OF CANADA
THE LAND AND PEOPLE OF CENTRAL AMERICA
THE LAND AND PEOPLE OF CEYLON
THE LAND AND PEOPLE OF CHILE
THE LAND AND PEOPLE OF CHINA
THE LAND AND PEOPLE OF COLOMBIA
THE LAND AND PEOPLE OF THE CONGO
THE LAND AND PEOPLE OF CUBA
THE LAND AND PEOPLE OF CZECHOSLOVAKIA
THE LAND AND PEOPLE OF DENMARK
THE LAND AND PEOPLE OF EGYPT
THE LAND AND PEOPLE OF ENGLAND
THE LAND AND PEOPLE OF ETHIOPIA
THE LAND AND PEOPLE OF FINLAND
THE LAND AND PEOPLE OF FRANCE
THE LAND AND PEOPLE OF GERMANY
THE LAND AND PEOPLE OF GHANA
THE LAND AND PEOPLE OF GREECE
THE LAND AND PEOPLE OF THE GUIANAS
THE LAND AND PEOPLE OF HOLLAND
THE LAND AND PEOPLE OF HUNGARY
THE LAND AND PEOPLE OF ICELAND
THE LAND AND PEOPLE OF INDONESIA
THE LAND AND PEOPLE OF IRAN
THE LAND AND PEOPLE OF IRAQ
THE LAND AND PEOPLE OF IRELAND
THE LAND AND PEOPLE OF ISRAEL
THE LAND AND PEOPLE OF ITALY
THE LAND AND PEOPLE OF JAPAN
THE LAND AND PEOPLE OF JORDAN
THE LAND AND PEOPLE OF KENYA
THE LAND AND PEOPLE OF KOREA
THE LAND AND PEOPLE OF LEBANON
THE LAND AND PEOPLE OF LIBERIA
THE LAND AND PEOPLE OF MALAYSIA
THE LAND AND PEOPLE OF MEXICO
THE LAND AND PEOPLE OF MOROCCO
THE LAND AND PEOPLE OF NEW ZEALAND
THE LAND AND PEOPLE OF NIGERIA
THE LAND AND PEOPLE OF NORWAY
THE LAND AND PEOPLE OF PAKISTAN
THE LAND AND PEOPLE OF PERU
THE LAND AND PEOPLE OF THE PHILIPPINES
THE LAND AND PEOPLE OF POLAND
THE LAND AND PEOPLE OF PORTUGAL
THE LAND AND PEOPLE OF RHODESIA
THE LAND AND PEOPLE OF ROMANIA
THE LAND AND PEOPLE OF RUSSIA
THE LAND AND PEOPLE OF SCOTLAND
THE LAND AND PEOPLE OF SIERRA LEONE
THE LAND AND PEOPLE OF SOUTH AFRICA
THE LAND AND PEOPLE OF SPAIN
THE LAND AND PEOPLE OF SWEDEN
THE LAND AND PEOPLE OF SYRIA
THE LAND AND PEOPLE OF TANZANIA
THE LAND AND PEOPLE OF THAILAND
THE LAND AND PEOPLE OF TURKEY
THE LAND AND PEOPLE OF URUGUAY
THE LAND AND PEOPLE OF VENEZUELA
THE LAND AND PEOPLE OF ZAMBIA

The Land and People of the
ARABIAN PENINSULA

by Mary Louise Clifford

PORTRAITS OF THE NATIONS SERIES

J. B. LIPPINCOTT COMPANY
Philadelphia   New York

For the use of the photographs on the following pages, the author gratefully credits:
  Abu Dhabi Petroleum Company, Ltd.: 24, 80, 109, 142, 152, 153
  Arabian American Oil Company: 19, 21, 32, 47, 54, 58, 73, 81, 102, 132, 165, 167, 173
  Caltex Petroleum Company: 39, 51, 91, 183
  Continental Oil Company: 118, 159
  Gulf Oil Corporation: 123
  International Graphics Printing Service: 113
  Kuwayt Ministry of Information: 40, 69
  Kuwayt Oil Company: 87, 147, 180
  Ministry of Information, Sultanate of Oman: 136
  Qatar Ministry of Information: 66, 94, 126
  United Nations/FAO/F. Mattioli: 29

U.S. Library of Congress Cataloging in Publication Data

Clifford, Mary Louise.
  The land and people of the Arabian Peninsula.

  (Portraits of the nations series)
  Includes index.
  SUMMARY: An introduction to the geography, history, government, natural resources, culture, and people of the eight nations that occupy the Arabian Peninsula.
  1. Arabia—Juvenile literature. [1. Arabia] I. Title.
  DS204.C54   953   76-49576
  ISBN-0-397-31685-2

Copyright © 1977 by Mary Louise Clifford
All Rights Reserved
Printed in the United States of America
2 4 6 8 9 7 5 3 1

Map by Donald T. Pitcher

To Bob

Contents

	The Eight Nations of the Arabian Peninsula	11
1	Desert	17
2	The People	28
3	Past	38
4	Islam	64
5	Language	71
6	Customs	78
7	Nationhood	97
8	Politics	116
9	Oil	139
10	Development	161
11	Values	176
	Index	187

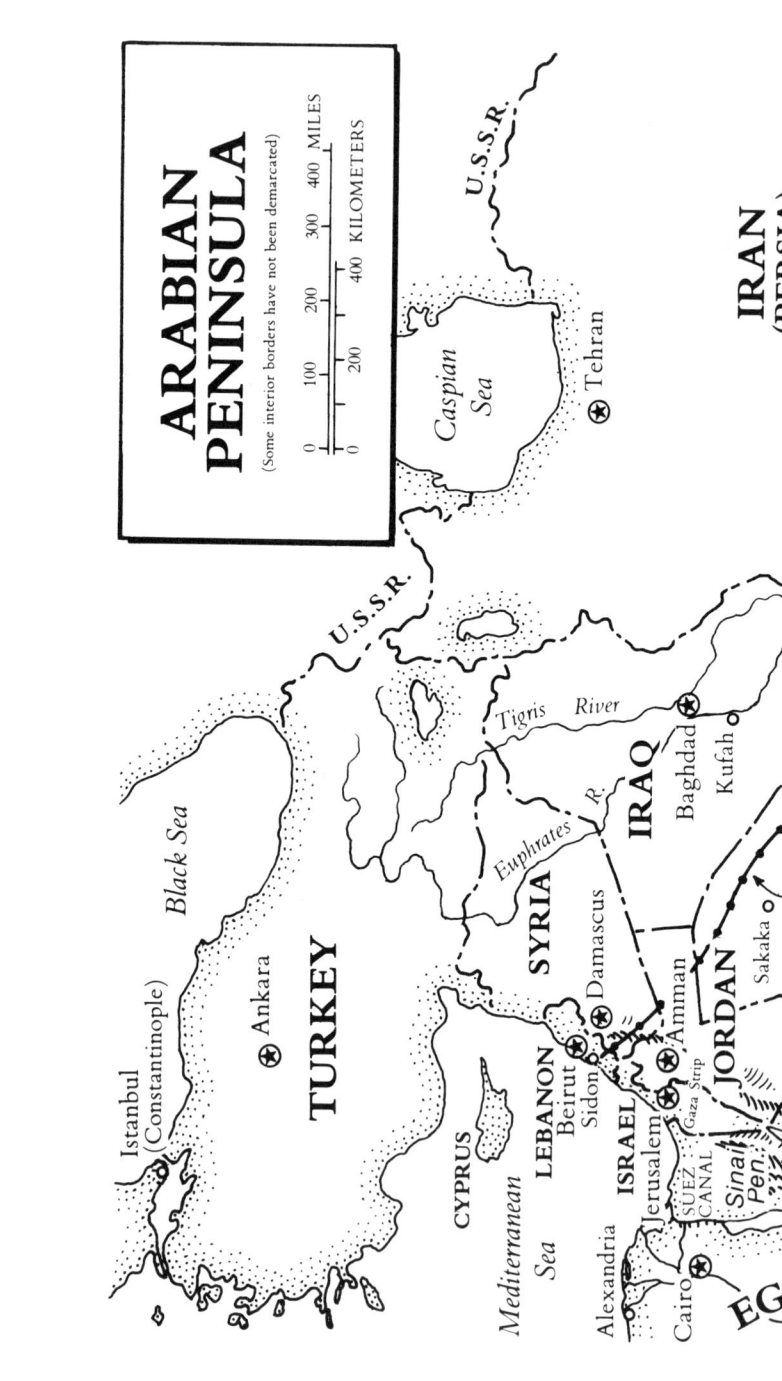

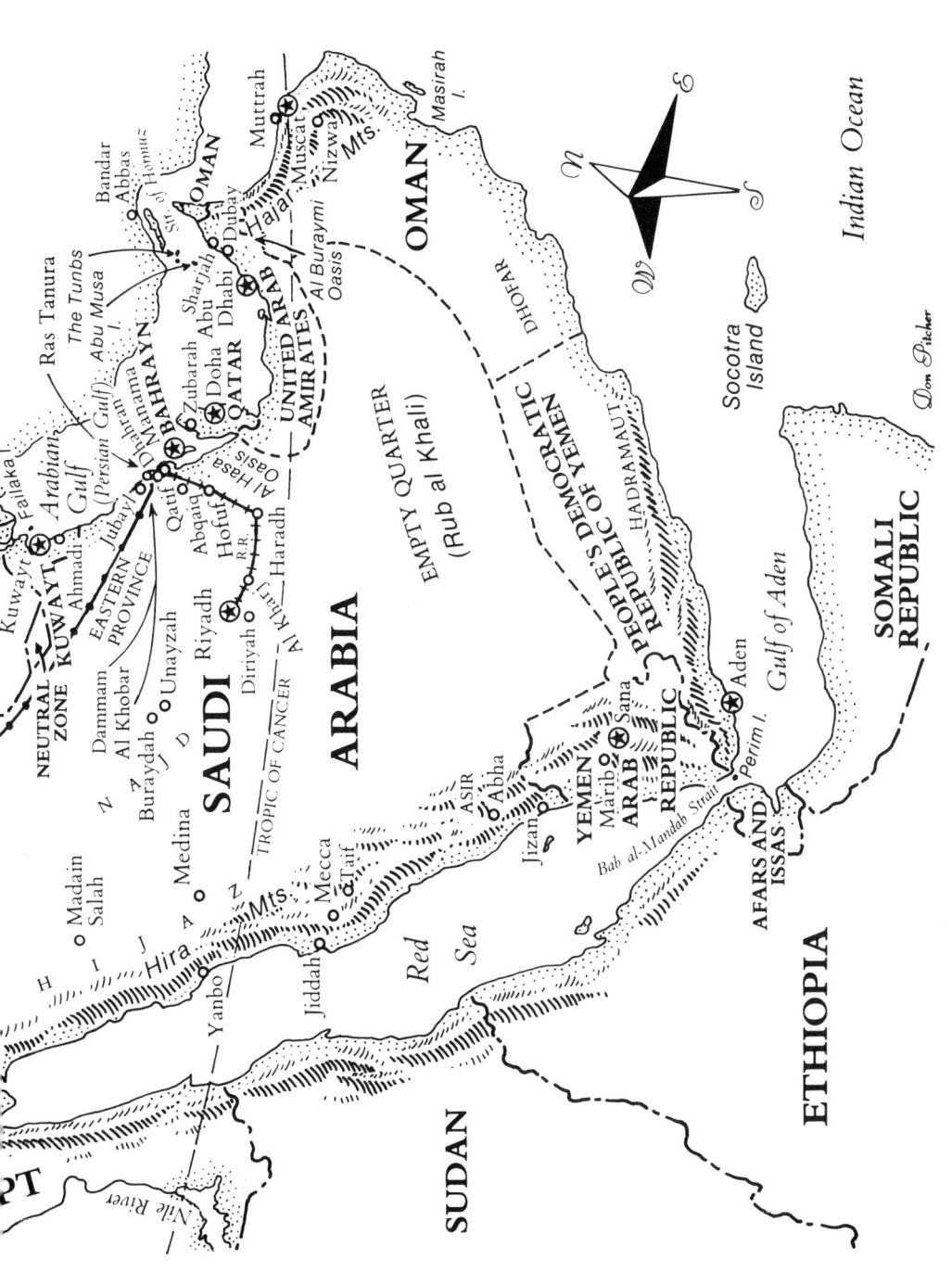

The Eight Nations of the Arabian Peninsula

THE YEMEN ARAB REPUBLIC

Area: 75,000 square miles (about the size of Nebraska)
Population: 6 to 7 million (1973 estimate)
Capital city: Sana
Government: Presidential Council (largely military) with a prime minister and cabinet appointed by the Council
Economy: Subsistence farming on well-watered, terraced mountain slopes; exports small amounts of coffee, *qat* (a mildly narcotic plant), cotton, rock salt; remittances from over a million Yemenis working in other Arab countries
Average annual per capita income (total national income divided by total population): $120 (1974 World Bank estimates used)

THE PEOPLE'S DEMOCRATIC REPUBLIC OF YEMEN

Area: 112,000 square miles (about the size of Arizona)
Population: 1.5 million (1972 estimate)
Capital city: Aden

Government: Radical socialist republic, administered by a three-man Presidential Council, aided by a ten-man executive committee of the only political party, the National Liberation Front

Economy: British oil refinery at Aden uses imported crude; subsistence farming and herding in very dry interior

Average annual per capita income: $120

OMAN

Area: Between 82,000 and 100,000 square miles (interior borders undelineated; about the size of Oregon)

Population: 750,000 (1972 estimate)

Capital city: Muscat

Government: Absolute monarchy; appointed ministers; Moslem law

Economy: Modest oil resources since 1964; construction; fish processing; subsistence farming and herding

Average annual per capita income: $1,250

SAUDI ARABIA

Area: Approximately 873,000 square miles (few borders with neighbors have been fixed; size of Texas and Alaska combined)

Population: 5.4 million (1974 estimate)

Capital city: Riyadh (population 350,000 in 1972)

Government: Monarchy, advised by an appointed council of ministers and an appointed Consultative Council; Moslem law, plus codified civil law in areas not covered by Moslem law

Economy: World's largest oil reserves; oil refining, natural gas, petrochemicals, fertilizer; construction; re-

THE EIGHT NATIONS OF THE ARABIAN PENINSULA 13

lated and light industries; both subsistence and irrigated farming and livestock production

Average annual per capita income: $2,080

KUWAYT (Kuweit)

Area: Between 6,000 and 8,000 square miles (size of New Jersey)

Population: 925,000 (1974 estimate; over half foreigners)

Capital city: Kuwayt

Government: Constitutional monarchy (constitution suspended in 1976)

Economy: Enormous oil resources; oil refineries, petrochemicals, fertilizer, ammonia; construction; shipping; light industries

Average annual per capita income: $11,640

BAHRAYN (Bahrein)

Area: Archipelago of one large and thirty-two small islands

Population: 230,000

Capital city: Manama

Government: Constitutional monarchy

Economy: Modest oil resources; oil refining; aluminum smelter; light industry

Average annual per capita income: $2,250

QATAR

Area: About 6,000 square miles (smaller than New Jersey)

Population: 140,000 (1974 estimate)

Capital city: Doha (Al Dawhah)

Government: Traditional Islamic monarchy

Economy: Substantial oil resources since 1940; petrochemicals, fertilizer, liquified natural gas; market gardening

Average annual per capita income: $5,830

UNITED ARAB AMIRATES (Emirates)

Area: About 32,000 square miles (a little larger than Maine)

Population: 650,000 (1976 estimate; over half foreigners)

Capital city: Abu Dhabi

Government: Constitutional federation of seven shaykhdoms, with president and vice president elected from among the shaykhs

Economy: Abu Dhabi has enormous oil resources, discovered 1958; Dubay (Dubai) has extensive oil resources, discovered 1967, plus fresh water for oasis farming; well developed port facilities for export trade; Sharjah has very modest oil resources, discovered 1970. The other four shaykhdoms (Ras al Khaymah, Umm al Qaywayn, Ajman, and Fujayrah) are very poor, depend on subsistence farming and herding, local fishing. Abu Dhabi pays most of federation expenses.

Average annual per capita income: $13,500

The Land and People of the
ARABIAN PENINSULA

1

Desert

Arabia—land of the Arabs. Does the word also mean exotic, mysterious, hidden treasure, magic genii, glittering palaces where veiled women dance behind pierced screens while incense perfumes the air and jewels glint in the flicker of hanging lamps? These are images straight out of *The Arabian Nights*, or *The Thousand and One Nights*—the tale of Scheherazade, who nightly regaled the Sultan Shahriyar of Persia with unfinished dramatic episodes to ensure his continued interest until he fell in love with her.

The some two hundred stories the clever lady told were folk tales of the time, gathered from Persia, India, Mesopotamia, and Egypt. The Sultan's court was patterned on that of the Moslem Caliph Harun al-Rashid, and was located in Baghdad rather than in Arabia. A Frenchman translated the stories in the 1700s and introduced them to Europe. They soon became world famous.

The images these stories evoke are of the luxury-loving Baghdad court of the tenth century, where music and art and literature and dance engrossed the rulers and exotic goods came from every corner of the known world to please their tastes. The stories are international. Aladdin was a poor Chinese boy in a Persian story who found a genie (from the Arabic *jinni*) in a lamp. Sinbad was a composite of dozens of Arab sailors who plied the Indian Ocean and visited spots as remote as Madagascar.

The Arabian Peninsula was almost as remote from wealthy, exotic Baghdad of the tenth century as Madagascar—at least in atmosphere. The Arabs of Arabia were living in goats' hair tents rather than palaces at that time. Their *jinn* were devils of the desert, created out of smokeless flame. Scheherazade's stories were recounted in the most beautiful city of the period, surrounded by the fertile farmland of the Tigris-Euphrates Valley. They told nothing of the blazing sun or blowing sand of Arabia, of the long slow treks by camel caravan across endless bleak landscapes, of hunger and thirst and the constant struggle to survive in the barren desert. The image of Arabia which they handed down to us had little to do with reality.

Sun and sand dominate the Arabian Peninsula. Although this large land mass is bounded on three sides by water—to the west the Red Sea; to the south the Gulf of Aden which is part of the much larger Indian Ocean; to the east the Arabian (Persian) Gulf—it is part of a great desert region that extends all the way from the Atlantic coast of North Africa to the Indian Subcontinent.

This is the largest peninsula in the world, about 1.2 million square miles—an area as big as the entire United States east of the Mississippi River. Much of it has little or no rainfall, and resembles Arizona and New Mexico. The very limited amount of available water is what makes a desert. The usual definition is any area which receives less than five inches of rain in a year's time.

Such desert areas are found generally in the latitude of the Tropic of Cancer and the Tropic of Capricorn (23°27'), which are the boundaries of the tropic zone, the farthest limit from the Equator where the sun can appear directly overhead. Although scientists are not exactly sure why, a belt of high barometric pressure forms around the earth near 30° latitude. Winds in a high pressure area spiral outward and downward, causing clouds to evaporate and bringing fair weather. The thirtieth parallel North coincides with the northern edge of the Arabian Peninsula.

There are some parts of the Arabian Peninsula which are

Mountain ranges in the Asir area of Saudi Arabia.

not desert, located along the coasts in the southwest part of the Peninsula. Here there are mountains that catch moisture-laden clouds blown over water, and by forcing them to rise and cool, make them condense and drop their moisture as rain. Some of these mountains in Yemen and in Asir Province of Saudi Arabia have snow on their peaks in winter, even though they are within the tropical zone.

Like Arizona and New Mexico, the desert of the Arabian Peninsula is not without water, even though it seldom rains. There are river systems that flow seasonally out of the mountains where rainfall is heavier, and although the water of these rivers disappears very rapidly through the porous desert sand, it is still there to be tapped, in basins of impervious rock lying below. There are also deep underground water sources—as there are under all land masses—trapped between layers of rock. Some of these are close enough to the surface that springs break through or wells can be dug by hand to reach them, and the Arabs have utilized these for centuries. Other sources are buried much deeper in the rock strata and can only be reached by drilling deep wells with complex mechanical equipment.

Once such underground sources of water are located and the water can be brought to the surface, then desert soils can be cultivated, for they are very fertile in many areas. The Al Hasa Oasis in the Eastern Province of Saudi Arabia, for example, is the largest oasis in the world. Fifty thousand acres of farmland there support 160,000 people. This has been a major oasis since time immemorial, fed by many natural springs which have recently been supplemented by artesian wells and modern irrigation networks.

Important sources of underground water have also been recently located in central Saudi Arabia, permitting a large

Aerial view of the city of Hofuf, in the Eastern Province of Saudi Arabia, which is located in the world's largest oasis.

cattle-growing project at Haradh, while at Al Kharj, where one of Saudi Arabia's first experimental farms was established in the late 1940s, huge fields of melons and market gardens stretch from horizon to horizon. Dams are being constructed in the southern mountains at Abha and in the Jizan valley to capture and control the runoff of rain water from the mountains and so increase the area of irrigated land. In the northern part of Saudi Arabia, at Unayzah and Buraydah, barriers of tamarisk and eucalyptus trees planted long ago bar drifting sand from an important farming area, where date palms and vegetable gardens provide food for people beside alfalfa fields which supply fodder for large herds of camels, sheep, cows, and chickens. Orchards of citrus fruits, peaches, apricots, and pomegranates are being planted near new grape vineyards. In the oil region of the Peninsula the windward side of dunes has been sprayed with asphalt to stabilize them and keep them from overrunning oases.

Rainfall in the desert varies, of course. Some years there is none at all, while others bring the blessing of more than the average two to four inches. Rains were particularly heavy in the winter and spring of 1975, and were considered a very good omen for the beginning of the reign of King Khalid in Saudi Arabia.

Large areas of the Peninsula consistently lack sufficient water for cultivation. Some of the region is pocked by barren stony mountains, the plains below cluttered with great boulders that have washed down from the highlands over the ages. An even larger area is sifted over by great dunes of drifting sand, the accumulated erosion of centuries of fierce winds blowing across empty landscapes with no green plant cover to break the wind's force or hold the soil in place. As the centuries pass the rocks break up into smaller and smaller particles, scattering great plains with gravel, until finally they are ground into drifting sand which sifts in endless undulating ribbons and ridges across fields of rock and flat white plains.

One large region in the south central part of the Arabian Peninsula is so dominated by massive shifting dunes of sand, hundreds of feet high, that it is called the Empty Quarter (*Rub al Khali*). It is the largest uninterrupted mass of sand in the world, covering 250,000 square miles, an area almost as large as Texas. No one ventured into that desolate wasteland save the hardy Bedouin and his incredibly tough camels until the later 1960s, when helicopters and fat-tired desert trucks made it possible for geologists to begin searching there for oil.

No desert is completely barren or empty, however. Even in the Empty Quarter a good rain every three or four years is enough to sustain a particularly hardy species of salt grass, which provides fodder for the single-humped dromedary camel. The Bedouin drive their beasts from water hole to water hole, traveling twenty or thirty miles a day, and the camels drink thirty gallons of water at once to sustain them through the long trek to the next water source. Their masters drink camel milk to survive through the long waterless days.

Other animals can also survive in the desert because of their ability to run swiftly and cover the long distances between water sources. There are two types of antelope in the Arabian desert—the small, fleet gazelle, and the large, stately (and now almost extinct) oryx. Fox, lynx, wolves, hyenas, wildcats, cheetahs, jackals, and an occasional leopard live in the less dry regions. Animals which burrow and so escape the desiccating heat of midday, like hedgehogs, hares, and hyraxes also survive, as do reptiles and lizards, which are cold-blooded and do not sweat. Ostriches were once found in the Peninsula, but are now extinct. Flamingos and pelicans are common where water is available, as are smaller birds such as the bulbul in oases and shore birds along the coasts.

Where a few inches of rain fall each year, a surprising amount of vegetation relieves the landscape, all of varieties which are either spiny-leaved—like juniper, aloe, and tamarisk—to expose a minimum of leaf surface to the burning rays of the sun, or water-storing plants like euphorbias and cacti. Fast-growing grasses spring up after even a light rain, maturing very quickly and dropping their seeds, which can survive through the long dry months until another rain comes

Great sand dunes surround an oasis in Abu Dhabi, one of the United Arab Amirates.

to sprout new growth. When it does rain, the desert is painted almost overnight with drifts of green seedlings, and this desert vegetation provides grazing for camels, goats, sheep, cattle, and the swift Arabian horse.

Where permanent water sources are available, reeds grow in profusion and provide thatch for house roofs. The date palm is the most important cultivated plant in desert oases, providing food, wood for fires, and leaves for roof thatch and baskets.

Without adequate supplies of water, however, large areas of the Arabian Peninsula can support only livestock and nomads. About fourteen million people live in this very large land mass but half of these are concentrated in the two Yemens in the southwest corner of the Peninsula, where rainfall is heaviest. In the rest of the Peninsula the population is so spread out that the provision of social services like roads, schools, and hospitals is very expensive.

Natural resources have until recently been very limited also, so that occupations have been predominantly farming in the watered areas and livestock grazing in the desert. However, the mid-twentieth century brought a concerted search for minerals, and a number have been located.

Most important, of course, is petroleum, the "liquid gold" that is found in various regions of the world that were once covered by ancient seas millions of years ago. Enormous reserves of petroleum are concentrated in the Gulf region because in prehistoric times the Gulf was a much larger sea, covering most of central Arabia and lands to the north, and teeming with plant and animal life. The sediments and marine deposits of the ancient sea were tilted eastward by a major geological upheaval which separated the Arabian Peninsula from the Sahara and formed the Great Rift Valley. Lava poured from cracks in the earth's surface and pushed up plateaus and volcanos, while land sank into the cracks to form a series of valleys that extend from Syria south through Africa all the way to Mozambique. The Arabian Peninsula today is a sort of vast table, heaved up at its western edge along the Red Sea by the geological faulting that formed the Rift. Mountains on the western and southern rim and in Oman in the far eastern corner of the Peninsula are the high side of the table, and drainage is from these high regions in a northeasterly direction toward the Gulf. The ancient shield that existed before the Rift is covered by layers of sediment which increase in thickness toward the Gulf. Petroleum has formed in the lower strata of these sedimentary layers and, like water, has trickled down into subterranean rock strata below the low basin that contains the Gulf.

Saudi Arabia has in its Eastern Province the largest petroleum reserves of any country in the world. Tiny Kuwayt, which is tucked into the northeastern corner of the Peninsula between Saudi Arabia and Iraq, ranks third. (The USSR is second.) Farther south along the Gulf coast the tiny shaykhdom of Abu Dhabi (one of the United Arab Amirates) ranks seventh in oil reserves, after Iran, the United States, and Iraq. Dubay and Sharjah, also members of the United Arab Amirates, have much smaller quantities of petroleum, as does the independent island of Bahrayn and the Sultanate of Oman.

The remaining two countries on the Peninsula, the Yemen Arab Republic and the People's Democratic Republic of Yemen, have discovered no oil. Their income is determined largely by the rainfall that waters farmland in fertile green valleys amid rolling hills and mountains.

These, then, are the countries of the Arabian Peninsula. Most of these countries are so newly independent that the interior boundaries between them and Saudi Arabia, which occupies the heart of the Peninsula, have not yet been demarcated. When attempts are made to draw them, they will run through remote, very inaccessible desert areas where the severe climate will make surveying extremely difficult and where the movements of traditionally nomadic pastoral tribes will lead to disputes over which new national government should control them.

2

The People

The people of the Arabian Peninsula are Arabs, but it is difficult to define exactly what an Arab is. The term itself—*arab*—means "desert dweller," and the Bedouin of the Arabian Peninsula call themselves *al-Arab*. However, there are millions of people who today call themselves Arabs and are certainly not nomads of the Arabian Desert.

The Arabian nomads spilled out of their desert fastnesses in the seventh century to spread Islam, the new religious faith preached by the Prophet Muhammad. Since one of the fundamental precepts of that faith was the brotherhood and equality of all men in the community of Islam, the separate ethnic identity of the Peninsula Bedouin soon got lost in the enormous racial diversity of people who adopted the Moslem religion. Along with the faith, they adopted the Arabic language, and as centuries of assimilation passed, all those people speaking Arabic as their native language came to call themselves Arabs. As a result, in modern times the designation *Arab* refers to a language group, not to an ethnic group or a single national community. It includes not only the people of the Arabian Peninsula, but also of Iraq, Syria, Jordan, Lebanon, Egypt, and most of North Africa.

Street scene in Sana, capital of the Yemen Arab Republic.

Arab mythology maintains that the Arabs are descended from Shem, the eldest son of Noah. The Arabs of the Peninsula divide themselves into two lineages, a custom that has matured and endured over several hundred years. The distinction may originally have risen between the settled farming peoples of the Yemen highlands, and the nomadic tribes to the north in the desert. The *Arab al Araba*, or pure Arabs, originated in the Yemen highlands and are descended from a legendary ancestor named Qahtan (or Joktan). His descendants today are called Qahtani, or southern Arabs, and dwell largely in Saudi Arabia and Yemen. The *Arab al Mustaraba,* or adopted Arabs, originated in the north and are called Adnani since they are descended from an ancestor named Adnan, the offspring of Ishmael, who was the son of the Biblical Abraham. Particular prestige adheres to the Adnani because one of their tribes, the Quraysh, produced the Arab Prophet Muhammad. The Adnani populate much of Saudi Arabia, Kuwayt, Bahrayn, Qatar, and the United Arab Amirates.

Accounts by ancient historians make it clear that nomadic merchants of the Arabian Peninsula were an important link in the caravan trade that transported silks and spices from India; ivory, animal skins, and slaves from Africa; semi-precious stones, gold, and possibly copper from Arabia itself to the commercial centers of ancient Egypt, Syria, and Mesopotamia. Large towns grew up as supply stops along caravan routes that were the forerunners of modern highways that crisscross the Peninsula today. And Arab *dhows* (small sailing ships with lateen rigging) plied the Gulf and Red Sea, carrying the exotic goods of India and Africa to ancient seaports like Muscat and Jiddah on the Arabian Peninsula.

Knowledge of these activities comes to us from other than Arab sources, however, for little was written in Arabic before Muhammad wrote the Islamic scriptures called the Koran in the seventh century. We can only conclude by inference that the very early Arabs of the Peninsula were nomadic tribes speaking a Semitic language, with perhaps a few established settlements at important commercial points and in the oases along the caravan routes.

These nomadic tribes continued their ancient way of life right into the twentieth century and are the people we know today as Bedouin (*Bedu* in Arabic—a term which means nomadic, camel-breeding tribes of the Arabian Desert). They comprise today perhaps only 10 percent of the population of the Arabian Peninsula, but before the development of the vast oil industry, the Bedouin predominated throughout the Peninsula. Their customs shaped the way of life there and come to the minds of most outsiders when we think of that part of the world. The Bedouin ethos is still regarded as the heroic ideal by most Arabs, in much the same way that Americans admire the spirit of the Old West.

Environment determined the Bedouin way of life. With too little water for settled agriculture, livestock became the key to survival. Movement from place to place was a necessity in order to find grass on which animals could graze. The extremely dry regions of the Arabian Peninsula sustain only the scantiest of scrub grass. The only animal that can cover the long distances between scattered patches of grass and also survive on meager sustenance without well or spring water to drink is the camel. This beast can go long periods without drinking because of its ability to tolerate wide ranges of body temperature without sweating heavily. Even the loss of a quarter of its body weight in water does not cause the fatal reduction in blood volume that kills other animals under great heat stress. It was the domestication of the one-humped dromedary camel—probably in the eleventh or twelfth century B.C.—that made possible the Bedouin way of life in the Arabian Desert.

Camels provided the Bedouin in the harshest desert regions with their essential necessities: transport, most vital of all; milk

Camel races are an annual event at Sakaka in northeastern Saudi Arabia.

to drink where there was no water, and occasionally meat; cloth of camel hair for their tents. The nomads added to these the dates gathered at the oases between which they traveled; wheat flour for unleavened bread, when they could find it; Persian carpets which served in place of beds, chairs, and tables. In the most hospitable areas where well water was available at regular intervals, a flock of goats supplemented their meager existence. And nature's every whim was turned to any advantage possible, as when a plague of locusts provided a roasted delicacy that varied the monotony of milk and dates for every meal.

Although there are very few Bedouins still practicing their ancient way of life, almost every Arab of the Peninsula today looks back proudly to the time of his Bedouin ancestors. Even though he may be a sophisticated town dweller, today's Arab has a nostalgic attachment to those traits most cherished by the stalwart nomads of the desert. If you ask Arabs what they consider their best qualities, they will probably mention hospitality and generosity, honor and honesty, friendliness and pride. All these traits are interrelated, and are a heritage from Bedouin background.

Bedouin social practices had their origin in very ancient times, long before the establishment of Moslem law. Bedouin custom may have shaped the first code of laws in history, that formulated by Hammurabi, king of Babylon about eighteen hundred years before Christ, which contained provisions regulating family affairs, loans and debts, false accusations, and individual rights that protect the weak from the strong. Hammurabi's code echoed the Bedouin's egalitarian attitude toward his fellow men, regardless of rank, and its provisions reflected the Bedouin practice of severely punishing individuals in order that the group might survive.

The high value the Bedouin placed on kinship ties and family honor stems from the harshness of desert life. Because existence in a desert environment is impossible for a lone individual, loyalty to kin and the tribe became the foundation of desert society. Any behavior necessary to ensure group survival in the desert was thought to be honorable; poverty made raiding unrelated tribes, sedentary neighbors, and passing caravans a necessity, and thus raiding became an honorable source of livelihood. Conversely, disloyalty to the family or tribe—acting contrary to the interests of the group—was considered dishonorable in the extreme, equivalent to treason.

Among the Bedouin desert dwellers, a man's name was often all the wealth he had, so he guarded fiercely the honor of his family name. The Bedouin code of honor, backed by public opinion, had the force of law. Because there was no central authority to impose the law, vengeance became the accepted way of redressing wrongs or erasing dishonor. The principle of vengeance—"An eye for an eye and a tooth for a tooth"—is clearly stated in the Old Testament, our written record of the ancient Middle East.

The ancient tribal codes were implemented by consent. They worked only when every individual was completely dependent on his kin group to survive. Punishment was ostracism or exclusion from the kin group, as good as a death sentence. Today, when a central government imposes law and order and the individual can support himself and his family by working for wages, the stern Bedouin code is no longer essential to provide a framework for Arabian society. Yet its emotional appeal is still very strong.

Islam, formulated in the seventh century, sanctioned the ancient Bedouin customs—seclusion of women to protect family honor, vengeance to redress stains on honor, severe punishment for individual crimes, an egalitarian belief in the brotherhood of man—and incorporated them into Moslem law. Indeed, the old tribal loyalties to kin and against outsiders proved stronger than the unifying effects of the Moslem religion, and led to the disintegration of the various Islamic states set up by the Moslem caliphs.

Both the tribal codes and Moslem law are deeply ingrained in Arab society today, particularly in the Arabian Peninsula. Moslem law is only now gradually being modified for modern usage through the codification of a new body of civil law, but an older generation is still alive which grew up scarcely touched by the outside world, and their sense of the fitness of traditional customs still prevails in the vast rural areas of the Peninsula. Even in urban areas kinship ties and pride in high moral standards are more openly demonstrated than in the West.

The Bedouin way of life is itself changing rapidly today. Bedouin families now often own pickup trucks. They hire tank trucks to bring water to the pastures so that animals no longer have to be driven from well to well to drink, and when they do need to move, they rent diesel trucks to transport their family members, their possessions, and their flocks of goats and sheep from pasture to pasture, leaving a few men to walk beside their camels. It is not at all unusual to see a motorcycle parked against a nomad tent.

Most Bedouin have already settled down in areas where farming or commerce provides an alternate way of life. This trend toward permanent settlement has been greatly accelerated in the last twenty-five years because revenues from petroleum have paid for all sorts of social services that make settled life more attractive than the old nomadic ways, and local rulers have actively encouraged settlement schemes to attract the nomads. The people of the Arabian Peninsula today are predominantly farmers and town dwellers, and the ways in which they gain their livelihoods are very different from the austere self-reliance that the desert imposed on the Bedouin.

The Peninsula has in the last twenty-five years undergone a transformation in living patterns unparalleled in history in its speed and scope, and the quarter century to come will witness a continued transformation of the same or even greater magnitude. Economic revolution made possible by oil revenues will change the face of the landscape beyond all belief. Will it also change the mind and heart of the Peninsula Arab beyond recognition?

The population of the Peninsula is almost all Moslem, speaks Arabic, and is relatively homogeneous because there has been limited immigration into the Peninsula except on the coasts and borders. Importation of slaves from Africa accounts for the occasional black-skinned citizen, particularly on the southwest coast in the Yemens, and Indian and Malayan traits are seen occasionally in the eastern regions.

The Moslems of the Peninsula represent both of the great sects of Islam, which resulted from a schism in the leadership of the faith in the ninth and tenth centuries. Orthodox Sunnis are in the great majority (90 percent in Saudi Arabia, for example), but Shia Moslems are concentrated in Yemen and in many communities in the Gulf region, where their special customs distinguish them from their neighbors. They are mostly farmers, farm laborers, and artisans, and have proven adept at filling positions in the oil industry.

The Sunni Moslems include the large landowners, the political leaders, and the Bedouin, and consider their social status superior to the Shias. Each group marries within its sect, and social barriers do exist, although no official discrimination between the two groups is sanctioned. However, the sheer preponderance of Sunni numbers frequently makes the Shias feel that they are victims of Sunni administrative preferences.

There are a fair number of non-Arab Moslems integrated into the population, particularly around Mecca and Medina where they came as Moslem pilgrims to the holy shrines of Islam and never left. There are large numbers of Arabs from neighboring countries resident in the Peninsula today, attracted by steadily growing job opportunities resulting from increasing oil revenues. Kuwayt is the most conspicuous example, with over 57 percent of its population foreigners, mostly Arabs, at least a fifth of them Palestinians. Egyptians, Jordanians, Iranians, Pakistanis, and Indians are also numerous. There are substantial numbers of non-Arab and non-Moslem foreigners as well, resident particularly in the commercial cities and the oil-producing regions of the Gulf. These are technicians, professionals, and businessmen from all over the world who have come to the Arabian Peninsula to fill the need for manpower skills and business initiatives which cannot be supplied locally. They are subject to Islamic law in exactly the same manner as local citizens.

There are no Jews left in the Peninsula today. Early Jewish residents of Mecca and Medina and the surrounding area were forced out during the spread of Islam in the seventh century. In the mountainous Asir region Jews were fairly numerous until the Wahhabi reform movement two hundred years ago. The last Jews, concentrated particularly in Yemen, moved to Israel after the Palestine War of 1947–48, and their presence in the countries of the Peninsula is officially forbidden as long as the Arab countries are at war with Israel.

3

Past

The earliest archeological remains that have been found in the Arabian Peninsula are on islands off the eastern shore, in the body of water we know as the Persian Gulf, but which the Arabs proudly call the Arabian Gulf. (To avoid wounding anyone's pride, people working in that area now call it simply "the Gulf.")

A port named Dilmun, located on Bahrayn Island, dominated the trade of the Gulf three thousand years before the birth of Christ, while the Sumerians were ruling the Tigris and Euphrates valleys. Dilmun, and probably similar cities located on Failaka Island off the coast of Kuwayt and in the Qatar Peninsula, were important trading links between Sumer and the Indus Valley civilization of that time (located in today's Pakistan). An enormous prehistoric cemetery of that period has been found at Dilmun on Bahrayn, containing over one hundred thousand tombs. Archeologists are finding similar traces today in Kuwayt, and are just beginning to unravel the history of civilizations that were flourishing at the same time as ancient Mesopotamia. Archeological evidence is also turning up in Oman, in the southeast corner of the Arabian Peninsula, suggesting that the people of that area were an-

Excavations at Bahrayn Fort on the Island of Bahrayn.

other link in this ancient international trade pattern. The Omanis may also have been the first people to domesticate the camel.

The Bible gives us our earliest written record of events in the Arabian Peninsula. The place called Ophir in the Bible was probably the western province of Oman, today called Dhofar. Ophir was an important source of myrrh and frankin-

Excavations at the site of a Greek temple found on Failaka Island, offshore from Kuwayt.

cense, fragrant gum resins from indigenous shrubs, which were highly prized by the Egyptians and Romans for religious ceremonies and cosmetic purposes.

The Old Testament also tells us that Saba was a prosperous trade link on the caravan route between the ports on the southern coast of Arabia and the Mediterranean. Ancient people called the Minaeans and the Sabaeans developed kingdoms in the well-watered mountains of the southwest corner of the Peninsula more than seven centuries before the birth of Christ. A Sabaean queen—the Queen of Sheba—paid a ceremonial visit to King Solomon in Jerusalem. Her capital, Saba, was located where the present town of Marib now stands, in the country which is today called the Yemen Arab Republic.

The Romans named the mountains of what is today Yemen *Arabia Felix* ("Happy Arabia") because it was blessed by plentiful rainfall in a region surrounded by oceans of sand. The local inhabitants centuries ago developed an advanced agricultural system based on terracing fields and on water control through dams, which provided irrigation. This region was also an important source of myrrh and frankincense.

In the second century B.C. both the Minaeans and the Sabaeans were supplanted by the Himyarite kingdom. Like that of its predecessors, its prosperity was based on control of the vital caravan route called the Incense Trail, which linked the Indian Ocean with the Mediterranean seaports. Not only myrrh and frankincense were eagerly sought by the Mediterranean peoples, but also the goods of India and Africa. Since there was no convenient sea route for the exchange of commodities, ships which plied the Indian Ocean unloaded their cargoes at ports in southern Arabia to be transported north by camel. Great caravans were made up semiannually, numbering a thousand camels and more. They moved across the desert wastes and through the rocky mountain valleys from waterhole to wellspring, where enormous tent cities sprang instantly to life when they camped and vanished just as quickly as they moved on. The tribes which controlled the watering places and owned the camels prospered on the fees they received.

From about 350 B.C. to 100 A.D. an Arab tribe called the Nabateans controlled the northern end of the Incense Trail. They left behind impressive stone-carved facades of temples and tombs, not only at Petra, their capital city located in today's Jordan, but also in northern Arabia at Madain Salah. Archeologists are at work today deciphering the clues in these ancient structures which will unfold the history of these long-forgotten people.

By the fifth century A.D. the Christian faith had spread both along the Red Sea coast of Arabia and into Abyssinia, that country in the horn of Africa which is today called Ethiopia. Abyssinian Christians helped Himyarite Christians (in today's Yemen) to overthrow their non-Christian ruler in 525, but the Abyssinians were soon driven out by invading Persians whose imperial power had already waxed and waned for many centuries. The great Marib Dam, which had been the heart of the complex irrigation system of the Yemen region, collapsed in 570, ending the once-great agricultural prosperity of the area.

The Persians also considered the Gulf coast of the Arabian Peninsula part of their maritime trading complex, but Persian domination was soon interrupted. The Prophet Muhammad was born in 570 in the Arabian city called Mecca, located around an important water source in the mountains that border the Red Sea. Arabia was populated by many separate and distinct tribes, each worshipping its particular deities. One whose origin was very ancient was called Allah, who was believed to be the creator, the provider, and the one who aided them in peril. Muhammad transformed that deity into the central focus of a faith which is embraced today by one-sixth of the world's total population.

Muhammad was a member of the aristocratic Quraysh clan which governed Mecca and cared for its major shrine, the Kaabah. Muhammad himself seems to have been obscure and impoverished, orphaned at an early age, and apparently brought up by a grandfather. We know little of his youth except that he was employed in his twenties to manage the caravans of a wealthy widow, who had inherited a thriving commercial business. Although the widow Khadija was much older than Muhammad, he married her when he was twenty-four, and led the life of a well-to-do merchant thereafter.

Then, when he was about forty, Muhammad became so troubled by the social inequities and religious practices of the Meccan townsmen that he turned most of his attention to religious study. While he was meditating, he began having visions that God had chosen him to be the prophet who would teach the true religion to his people. God's messages, transmitted to Muhammad by the Archangel Gabriel, continued throughout Muhammad's life and were later incorporated into the holy book of Islam, the Koran (Qur'an in Arabic).

Muhammad's doctrine, when he began preaching, was a very simple instruction that the Arabs should abandon their many idols and worship only one God. The message was parallel to that of both the Jewish and Christian faiths. There were important Jewish colonies scattered throughout the Arabian Peninsula in Muhammad's time, and Jews seem to have dominated the commercial life of the area known as Hijaz, of which Mecca was the central city. Christianity was also widespread along the edges of Arabia, particularly in Syria, in the Hira Mountains to the northeast of Mecca, and in Yemen.

Muhammad's first converts were his wife and a cousin named Ali, who married his daughter and years later became one of his successors in leadership of the Moslem faithful. Gradually, as Muhammad expanded his message to emphasize the brotherhood and equality of all those who embraced Islam, he gathered converts from the poor and slave classes of Mecca. The merchant aristocracy of the city, particularly Muhammad's own Quraysh clan, soon became alarmed because the city thrived on the commerce connected with the worship of pagan gods and the profitable pilgrimages to their shrines. Muhammad's condemnation of these cults seemed to threaten Quraysh prosperity.

After a decade of ridicule and persecution, Muhammad escaped the opposition of the Meccan leaders by accepting an invitation from a group in Medina, 250 miles to the northeast, to make that city his home. About two hundred of his followers moved quietly from Mecca to Medina, and Muhammad followed in 622. This event, the first certain date in Moslem history, has been known by Moslems ever since as the Hegira (from the Arabic *hijrah,* meaning "migration"), and serves as the starting year of the Moslem calendar.

The Medinese who had extended the invitation to Muhammad were particularly interested in his leadership ability, for they needed someone with forceful character to referee the disputes among the clans that were wracking their city. Muhammad assumed the powers of governor of his small Moslem community, and considerably enhanced his prestige by making an accommodation with the large Jewish community in Medina. He added customs of Jewish ritual to his own cult, setting aside a Sabbath day of public worship, publicly calling his followers to three daily prayers, and instructing all Moslems to turn toward Jerusalem as they prayed. However, Muhammad's ignorance of Old Testament scripture soon made the Jews scornful, and he turned away from them when they would not accept his claim that his revelation came directly from God.

Muhammad then developed a pre-Hebrew source for his doctrine, adopting Abraham as the patriarch of Islam. According to Arab tradition, the Arabs are descended from Abraham's first son Ishmael, while the Hebrews are descended from his second son Isaac. The Prophet Muhammad traced back to Abraham the foundation of the Meccan sanctuary where the Kaabah stands, and sought to purify Mecca of all the pagan idols which had been added since Abraham. He changed his day of prayer to Friday, appointed a professional "cryer" (*muezzin*) to call the faithful to prayer instead of using trumpets and bells, and decreed a month of fasting (Ramadan) and an annual pilgrimage to the Kaabah in Mecca as Pillars of the Moslem Faith.

Muhammad quickly gained converts from many of the Arabian tribes, but he needed more than authority for his community to thrive. Economic resources for his people were secured by successfully raiding rich caravans moving to and from Mecca, and the wealth gained from these raids was attributed to divine providence.

The merchants of Mecca fought several disastrous battles against these attacks on their caravans, but were no match for the zealous Moslems. Finally in 628 they negotiated a ten-year truce which gave the Moslems the right to make their annual pilgrimage to the Kaabah in Mecca. However, in 630 Muhammad used the murder of a Moslem pilgrim as an excuse to break the truce, and his forces invaded and occupied the city. He immediately destroyed all the pagan relics in Mecca except for the large black meteorite which was housed in the Kaabah.

Now Muhammad turned away from both Jews and Christians and openly declared a new Arab religion. He decreed that prayers would henceforth be toward Mecca rather than Jerusalem, and that the Kaabah in Mecca was the center of the new faith and the focus of its pilgrimage.

The Prophet died two years later, at the peak of his career, triumphant in the city of his birth and recognized as the head of a powerful and growing community, tied together by monotheism and focused through a revealed scripture of his personal composition. The fragmented Arab tribes had needed a simple doctrine that could unify them and replace the multiple rivalries of idol worship and clan conflict. The earlier monotheistic faiths, Judaism and Christianity, had been spreading around the fringes of the Arabian Peninsula, but their codes were more suited to settled people and were more demanding than the individualistic Bedouin could easily accept. Muhammad offered a simple ethical ideal in the form of a commandment from God that required no great break with traditional Bedouin customs. It involved no complex theology, no priesthood, no hierarchy, no allegiance except to God. Every man who abandoned the crass materialism and fierce rivalry that was the rule of the time could become holy, and any man could be an *imam*, or leader of prayers. All that was required of him was that he profess his belief in the one true God.

Within a century after Muhammad's death, the Arab tribes had spilled out of the Arabian Peninsula to conquer an empire which stretched from the Atlantic to the Indus River, an expansion that probably surprised the conquerors as much as the conquered. Nothing about it was planned. Islam forbade the tribes who had embraced the faith to fight with each other, and so they simply turned their faces outward and directed their highly developed martial skills against their neighbors.

The movement began immediately after Muhammad's death. No sons survived him, nor did he make any provision for succession to his position as head of the Moslem community. Muhammad's close relatives of the Quraysh clan of Mecca stepped in and supported his elderly and pious father-in-law, Abu Bakr, as his *khalifah* or successor (caliph in English). But the Arabian tribes whom Muhammad had converted regarded their allegiance as personal to him. When he

Interior of the Holy Mosque of Medina, the city where the Prophet Muhammad is buried.

died, they considered that chapter closed and went their own separate ways again. Abu Bakr had to use military force to gather them back into his realm, and so he set in motion a military campaign that established his control over most of the Arabian Peninsula.

Once the Arabian tribes were united under one banner, they began raiding beyond their own borders, using horse and camel cavalry which were marvelously mobile and proved devastating in open country. The border tribes in Iraq, Syria, and Egypt were far too disorganized to resist this new form of guerilla warfare, and the Arabians moved easily into the provinces of Sasanid Persia and Greek Orthodox Byzantium, the two great empires to the north. Military conquest was not directed by the caliph in Medina. Each time his military commanders in the field met with success, they made simple on-the-spot decisions as to where to launch their next thrust. Often local inhabitants suggested the next move, and joined the Arabian tribes in raids against their oppressive rulers. These lightning strikes created chaos among the organized military forces of the Persians and the Byzantines.

These spontaneous campaigns brought rich rewards in booty and tribute to the warriors, and spurred enthusiasm for the Moslem faith. Islam provided the rallying cry and the unifying force to make the tribes fight together, but these early excursions into the borderlands were raids in search of loot rather than holy wars to spread the Moslem religion. It was a hundred years before the conquered peoples asserted themselves, became Arabs and Moslems, and took over the Islamic empire.

Abu Bakr died in 634, and his successor Caliph Umar (Omar), also a member of the Prophet's inner circle, set about systematically organizing military and religious and civil affairs. He instructed his followers to preserve Muhammad's revelations by writing them down in a holy book that became the Koran. He established a civil administration and pressed the military expansion of his realm.

Caliph Umar carried his campaigns first into Syria, besieging its most important city, Damascus, for six months and taking it by deceit in 635. The army Byzantium sent against him in 636 was thoroughly defeated, opening Syria completely to Moslem occupation. Iraq was taken in the same way in 637 and Jerusalem in 638, giving the Moslem invaders control of the heartland of the Fertile Crescent, the rich farming area that stretches from the Nile Valley across the Middle East to the Tigris-Euphrates Valley. The Arabians' momentum swept them eastward, across Persia, through what is today Afghanistan, and by 643 to the Indus River in what is now Pakistan.

If the coastline of Syria was to be held, the Arabians had to control Egypt, which was a major maritime province of Byzantium, ruled from Constantinople. In 640 an Arabian army besieged and took Alexandria, the Egyptian capital founded nine hundred years earlier by Alexander the Great. In Egypt too the local population welcomed the Arabian invaders as a relief from the tyranny of their Byzantine rulers.

Arabian morale was at its peak, borne forward beyond the Moslems' wildest imaginings by the vitality of their new faith. However, in all of these campaigns the tribes fought as separate, discrete units. Each followed its own banner, borne aloft on a lance by one of the bravest. They fought with the hardy endurance learned from long marches through the hostile Arabian Desert. They set up separate tribal encampments on their battlefields and separate quarters in the conquered towns. (The city of Cairo is an outgrowth of an Arabian military quarter called Fustat, located up the Nile rather than at

Alexandria.) Municipal government of conquered towns consisted of councils of chiefs drawn from the various tribal quarters.

The leaders of the new Moslem society were jealous of their privileges and prerogatives, especially when it came to naming a new caliph. Abu Bakr and Umar had been of Muhammad's own Hashemite family of the Quraysh tribe. When Umar died, the rival Umayyid family of the same aristocratic Quraysh tribe of Mecca succeeded in putting one of their members, Uthman (Othman), who had been a relative and close associate of the Prophet, into the caliphate. Uthman aroused strong jealousies by favoring relatives of his family in appointments to all important positions and controlling the central treasury into which all tribute was channeled. Arabian leaders in the provinces sent representatives from Egypt to Medina to negotiate, and eventually the caliph was murdered in 656. This event led to a rupture among Moslems that has never been mended, between those who believe that the caliph, as the Prophet's successor, should be of hereditary descent from Muhammad's inner circle of companions, and those who maintain that the protector of the Moslem faith should be elected from the Quraysh tribe and rule by consent, in the manner of a traditional Arabian chieftan.

The closest remaining member of the Prophet's inner circle was Ali, husband of Muhammad's daughter Fatima, but the Umayyid family refused to accept his election as caliph. Ali led a victorious army of conquest in Iraq and moved the seat of his caliphate from Medina to Kufah in Iraq. Arabian leaders in Syria who supported the Umayyids soon plotted against Ali, and accused him of complicity in Uthman's assassination. With the help of Arabian chiefs in Egypt, the governor of Syria forced Ali to negotiate. The next four years saw bitter fac-

The elaborate mosaic exterior of a mosque minaret in Manama, Bahrayn.

tionalism. Finally in 660 the Umayyids chose the Syrian governor, Muawiyah, to be their leader. Ali was assassinated a year and a half later, and his successor bought off. Muawiyah immediately moved the caliphate to Damascus.

Muawiyah was a man of great administrative skill. He developed an orderly organization for administering his realm and a disciplined army, which continued to push eastward and westward along the lines of least resistance, until his dominion eventually stretched all the way from Spain to Mongolia. He chose his son as his successor and thus established the principle of hereditary succession to the caliphate within the Quraysh tribe of the Prophet. When Muawiyah died, however, Ali's supporters (known by now as Shia) began agitating again to shift the caliphate back to Iraq and make Ali's second son Husayn (the Prophet's grandson) caliph instead of Muawiyah's successor. Husayn was killed in battle in 680. His martyrdom provided a focal point for all the grievances within the empire and particularly for clan rivalry between the Umayyids ruling in Damascus and the Hashemite family of the Prophet in Medina.

The battling between the clans over the next sixty years destroyed the unity of Moslem leadership. The Arabians split into warring factions, and their obsession with the quarrel gave rise to the distinction between northern and southern Arabs that persists today. The internal struggle was matched by a schism between the Persians, who were accustomed to a hereditary divine monarch and supported Ali, whom they regarded as the preeminent saint of Islam, and the Arabs who supported the Umayyids against the Arabs allied with the great clans of Medina. This schism also still persists, in the two great branches of Islam known as Shia and Sunni.

By the middle of the eighth century the Damascus caliphate

was no longer recognized outside Syria, and the caliph of this time was the last of the Umayyids. In 747 a revolt against the Umayyids was spearheaded by their cousins, the Abbas clan, now living in Persia. The Arabian tribes were too disunited to draw together. Umayyid power disintegrated, Umayyid family members were massacred in Damascus by the Abbas family, and the Abbasids appointed a caliph. This was, in effect, the end of Arabian control of the Moslem empire, for Arab blood was by now so mixed with that of the conquered peoples that a new society had emerged. The Arabian aristocracy was no longer necessary to the maintenance of the empire. For the next five hundred years Abbasid caliphs ruled the eastern empire from Baghdad, a new city of their own creation.

A similar process was going on to the west. The fall of Egypt had left the Byzantine provinces of North Africa open to Arab invasion. The Arabs succeeded over a period of many decades and after many reverses in imposing Islam on the Berbers of North Africa, and the Berbers in turn joined the forward rush of Islam. Berber soldiers were essential in carrying Islam to the Atlantic coast and in the armies that crossed from Morocco to conquer and rule Spain.

The existing Spanish regime had been tyrannical and had earned universal hatred, and internal strife permitted the Spanish cities to fall easily to the Moslem invaders. A Moslem province called *al-Andalus* (Andalusia) was swiftly established in the conquered territories. The forward movement of the Moslem armies in Europe finally came to a halt in France exactly a century after the Prophet's death, when the Arab-Berber forces were stopped in 732 in a battle between Poitiers and Tours. Moslem expansion had finally reached the point where it was so overextended and the Arab-Berber alliance worn so thin that it ran out of steam. Spain remained under

Pilgrims camp outside Mecca in western Saudi Arabia during the annual pilgrimage which all Moslems attempt to make at least once in their lifetime.

Moslem control for three centuries, and an illustrious branch of the Umayyid family ruled Spain from Cordova from 929 to 1031.

In the east, the further expansion of Islam after the eighth century was peaceful, carried out over a long period of time by itinerant traders, rather than by warriors, to the East Indies and south across the Sahara to black Africa.

The people the Arabs conquered were given a choice between paying tribute and being converted to Islam. Although the Moslem leaders did label their campaigns as *jihad* (holy war) in order to inspire their followers, the early Moslem invaders cared little about making converts. The Arabian warriors were quite happy to simply rule and receive tribute, which provided them with a source of substantial wealth. Before those who had been conquered could quit paying tribute, they had to become Moslems, which required them first to associate themselves with some Arab tribe. The material benefits of converting to Islam soon became clearly apparent to the subject peoples, and through the long process of Arabian expansion growing numbers of conquered inhabitants chose to learn Arabic, adopt Arab customs, and embrace the faith. Intermarriage, concubinage, and slavery accompanied the process quite naturally. Eventually the subjects outnumbered their Arab rulers and swamped the haughty Arabian aristocracy. It was not long before the egalitarian principles of Islam dissolved the distinctions between the two groups and both became part of a single Moslem Arab community, all speaking Arabic.

Moslem government was generally very tolerant of non-Moslems. The particularly benevolent rule of the Abbasids greatly encouraged wholesale conversions. Most of Moslem mission work was carried on peacefully, by converts rather than by Arabs.

The Abbasid caliphate proved to be the Golden Age of Islam, which was a legacy begun by the Moslems of Arabia, but not their creation. They had spilled out of the Arabian Desert and been absorbed by the peoples they conquered. The use of the Arabic language reached its zenith, but power was no longer in the hands of the Arabians. The Abbasid court was Persian, and Arabian tribal society was replaced by the centralized rule of an Oriental despot. The mixture of the brotherhood of Islam and the various cultures that were amalgamated into the Moslem Empire produced an age of science, literature, art, and architecture never surpassed. The period was one of enormous prosperity based on industry, agriculture, and farflung trade: in Saracen ships that sailed to East Africa, India, the East Indies, and China; by camel caravan across the Sahara to West Africa; and along the seas and rivers of Russia. But, spectacular as was the rise of the highly civilized Moslem Empire, so was its decline swift. By the middle of the tenth century, decadence, corruption, and intrigue had fragmented the realm to the point that the caliphate soon fell to pieces.

The center of the Empire had been moved from Medina to Damascus to facilitate administration of the growing realm, and then to Baghdad as Persian influence grew predominant. While Baghdad was reaching heights of wealth, intellect, and fame as a great center of culture, Arabia itself lapsed back into stagnation. The nomadic tribes reverted to their traditional rivalry and raiding, and remained politically fragmented for a thousand years.

In the fifteenth century Europe opened up sea routes to Asia around Africa, bypassing the Middle East and severing the important overland trade links between Europe and the East that had provided so much wealth to Middle Eastern merchants. When the Ottoman Turks conquered Egypt in 1517, they carried with them to Constantinople the last of the Abbasid line in order to establish the caliphate there. The Sultan of Turkey himself eventually assumed the caliphal privileges and title.

He rapidly took control of most of the Moslem Empire, including western Arabia, and even expanded Islam into the Balkans. However, with the end of the international trade that had provided continuous wealth there came a long period of commercial and intellectual stagnation. Because the Ottoman Turks were absorbed in wars with Austria, Russia, and Persia, the people of the Arabian Peninsula were left in their backwater to fend for themselves.

At about the same time that the Ottoman Turks took over control of the Moslem Empire, Europeans arrived in the Gulf. The Portuguese came first, in 1507, and changed the whole pattern of trade and power in the East. In 1515 they took control of the region called Muscat and Oman on the southeastern coast of the Peninsula, and remained until 1650 in spite of periodic revolts and conflicts with the local tribes. The Portuguese largely neglected the area and did little to develop its potential or the Gulf trade. In 1624 a strong Moslem imam (leader) was elected in Oman, and soon exerted his control over all of the interior.

By this time other European powers were entering the Gulf. The English defeated Portuguese fleets in 1610, 1615, and 1620, and helped the Persians eject the Portuguese from the island of Hormuz in 1622. In the early 1630s the Portuguese were absorbed in a conflict with the Dutch in India, and in the next twenty years the Imams of Oman took advantage of the Portuguese distraction to attack and seize all their ports in the Gulf.

Omani sailors had learned to sail and fight in Portuguese ships, and now they took to the seas themselves to harass the Portuguese. The Dutch and English joined the game with enthusiasm. Oman and Muscat were perfectly located for trading harbors, and the Omanis developed great maritime skill,

ranging the coasts of India and Africa and extending their control to Zanzibar and the other Portuguese settlements of East Africa.

By the 1670s piracy had become the dominant activity in the Gulf, and the Omanis competed expertly. The seaports gradually slid out of the control of the Imam, whose residence was at Nizwa in the interior mountains. By 1700 Muscat with its excellent natural anchorage had become a virtually independent city-state, thriving on plunder and customs duties forcibly levied on Gulf trade. Its bazaars were crowded with Socotra aloes, asafoetida, frankincense, putchok, and myrrh; minerals such as alum and sulphur; ivory from East Africa; fabrics and carpets from India; pearls from the Gulf; coffee from Mocha in Yemen. From Oman itself horses, livestock, fish, dates, fruits, vegetables, and cereals were available. In this era Muscat and Oman was the most powerful state in Arabia.

The Imams of Oman ruled supreme in the interior until 1719, when civil war broke out over the succession. A new dynasty gained control in 1728, its strength based on mercantile and maritime success rather than on spiritual leadership. By 1786 the ruler was styling himself Sultan and had moved his capital from Nizra to Muscat, leaving the interior under the religious control of the Moslem imam.

Meanwhile in the interior of the Arabian Peninsula the Bedouin tribes continued their age-old jockeying and rivalry for

For centuries graceful Arab dhows carried seamen to ports in Africa and Asia. They are now gradually being replaced by more modern craft.

power. In about 1710 several clans of the tribe called Atib (or Uteiba) moved from the interior Najd region of Arabia to escape drought and famine, and settled in Kuwayt, a small fishing village on the coast where the sea could supplement their food supply. These settlers were Sunni Moslems, cousins of the Al Saud family which would later unite Saudi Arabia. By the end of the century the Al Sabah clan of that tribe had established control of a small kingdom called Kuwayt under the leadership of their *amir* (prince). The Ottoman Turks recognized Al Sabah authority in 1756.

In 1766 the Al Khalifa family of the same tribe migrated south from Kuwayt and settled at Zubarah on the coast of the Qatar Peninsula. This town was the center of their thriving pearl trade until 1782, when the Al Khalifa attacked Bahrayn and established a dynasty there which still governs the Bahrayn Archipelago. This same family continued to control Qatar until it was occupied by the Turks in 1872, but they gradually moved from Qatar to Bahrayn in the face of attacks by militant Moslems from interior Arabia.

The Gulf region experienced a period of considerable disturbance in the nineteenth century when piracy was widespread along the Arabian coast. Great Britain intervened, ostensibly to subdue pirates and protect trade, and it was in this period that the many shaykhs (or *shaikhs, sheiks,* meaning "tribal chieftains") along the coast entered into treaty relationships which guaranteed British protection and excluded other foreign powers from the area.

In 1789 Britain signed an Agreement of Friendship with Oman, directed mainly at excluding the French from the Gulf. The British launched a campaign against the pirate strongholds on the coast between 1805 and 1818, which ended with a General Treaty of Peace in 1820 between Britain and the shaykhs in Bahrayn, Qatar, and the several fragmented shaykhdoms south of Qatar. This had to be supplemented in 1853 by a maritime truce, enforced by Britain, and it was at that time that the shaykhdoms south of Qatar became known as the Trucial Coast.

In 1839 Britain had captured the small fishing port of Aden, located on the southwestern tip of the Peninsula. Because of its strategic location, it grew into an important trading center and coal bunkering station, particularly after the opening of the Suez Canal in 1869.

To protect their vital interest in Aden, the British soon found it necessary to extend their control eastward into the area known as Hadramaut, and to develop treaty relationships with the many independent shaykhs of the hinterland. Sixteen shaykhdoms which accepted British protection became the Western Protectorate and four were included in the Eastern Protectorate, which included Hadramaut. Because of its commanding location at the entrance to the Indian Ocean on the route from Europe through the Mediterranean to the Orient, Aden became the most advanced of all the states of the Peninsula until World War II. The city was governed as a part of British India until it was made a separate British Crown Colony in 1937. British administration fostered the creation of various modern governing structures and a public school system, and prompted the growth of a strong trade union movement and the abandonment of traditional Moslem seclusion by many women.

While Britain was extending her influence along the Arabian coasts, a major modern reform movement was under way in the interior. In the early 1700s a Moslem religious leader from central Arabia decided to return his people to the strict and simple message of the Koran and the teachings of the

Prophet Muhammad. Shaykh Muhammad ibn Abd al-Wahhab had received a deeply religious education, and was determined to cleanse Islam of the festivals, pageantry, superstitions, mysticism, and saint-worship that the Shia Abbasids had added to it. His fanaticism led the local residents to drive him from his own home town, and he found refuge in Diriyah, not far from Riyadh, where the governing Al Saud family welcomed and supported him.

Shaykh Muhammad's followers were generally known as Wahhabis, and it was under the banners of this strict religious sect that the Saudi family conquered the tribes of central and western Arabia in the late 1700s and early 1800s. The Ottoman Turks countered by sending their allies, the Egyptians, to defeat the Wahhabis in 1818. Although the Bedouin had become nominal Moslems in the Prophet's time, they had never accepted the egalitarian philosophy of Islam and had refused to change their tribal way of life. Raiding, blood feuds, and vengeance continued to be their principal preoccupation until the twentieth century, when Abdul Aziz ibn Saud gathered them under his control, imposed law and order throughout his realm, and created the nation known as Saudi Arabia.

Even today the faith that is practiced in Saudi Arabia and the Gulf shaykhdoms is much stricter than that in other parts of the Moslem world. The Arabs who regard themselves as Wahhabis are the puritans of Islam. Moslem law is the basis of government; the prohibitions of the Koran are strictly observed; and social relationships are truly egalitarian. Saudi Arabia's association with the life of the Prophet and the presence of the holy cities of Mecca and Medina within its borders make Islam a primary force in shaping life and society. No non-Moslem ruler has ever, since Muhammad's time, controlled any of Saudi Arabia. No non-Moslem has visited the holy shrines except in disguise. Citizenship requires a declaration of the faith. Immigrants can convert to Islam, but Moslems do not repudiate their religion. They are particularly intolerant of agnosticism or atheism, for they find indifference to religion incomprehensible.

4

Islam

Moslem religious law governs society in the Arabian Peninsula, and government's function is to enforce Moslem law. Consequently, the outlook and ethics of the Peninsula Arabs are very much determined by the tenets of their faith. We must have some understanding of Islam if we are to understand Arab behavior.

The Arabian Peninsula was the birthplace of one of the world's great monotheistic religions, Islam, which means "submission to, or having peace with God." Those who believe in Islam are called Moslems (*Muslim* in Arabic), meaning "those who submit." Although the Prophet of Islam was Muhammad, his followers do not like to be called Muhammadans because that implies that they worship Muhammad. They do not; they worship only God, whom they call Allah (from the Arabic *al-ilah*, meaning "the Supreme Being").

Muhammad never claimed to have supernatural powers or to be anything more than an ordinary human being. He regarded himself simply as a man whom God had chosen to receive a perfected revelation of His will, which was now clarified through Muhammad and directed to his own people. However, no biography of Muhammad was written until 140 years after his death. Not surprisingly, by then his followers and succeeding generations of Moslems had ornamented his memory with a mantle of legend and mysticism far beyond anything that he intended. The pilgrimage (*hajj*) has always included a pious visit to his tomb in Medina.

Over 90 percent of Moslem theology is concerned with Allah. He has ninety-nine names and as many attributes, and the devout Moslem repeats them as he fingers his *subhah* or "worry beads." Using beads in prayer is a custom of Indian origin, which was adopted by the Sufi sect of Islam in about the ninth century to help recall the ninety-nine names of God. (Catholics started using the rosary in the thirteenth century, after the Crusades gave them contact with Moslems.)

The basic tenets of Islam are only five, and are known as the Pillars of the Faith. The first is the profession of the faith, which is all that is required to become a convert. *La ilaha illa Allah: Muhammadun rasulu Allah.* "There is no God but Allah: Muhammad is his messenger." These words are probably repeated more often than any other single phrase on earth.

The second pillar is prayer, and the faithful are called to prayer five times a day by the above phrase. At dawn, at midday, at mid-afternoon, at sunset, and early evening all good Moslems respond to the call of the *muezzin,* turn their faces toward Mecca, and recite their prayers, following prescribed ritualistic movements, which emphasize humility and devotion and also happen to be good exercise.

The third pillar of Islam is almsgiving, which originally was intended to support the poor among the Moslem community, to build mosques, and to defray administrative expenses. In some Moslem countries it is now left to one's conscience; in others it is collected as a tax (*zakat*).

The fourth pillar is fasting, a custom which was well es-

Moslem men pray in a mosque in Qatar.

tablished in Muhammad's time among both Christians and Jews. Muhammad prescribed the month of Ramadan as a time of total abstinence from food, drink, smoking, and sexual relations during the daylight hours. Since the Moslem calendar is based on the lunar cycle, Ramadan occurs at different times throughout the entire year. When it falls during hot summer months, fasting in desert countries is an act of real suffering and privation, and makes the Moslem aware of those in want.

The final pillar of Islam is pilgrimage, an ancient Arab tradition which Muhammad focused on the pilgrimage of Abraham to Mecca. Every Moslem, if he is able, is required to go once in his lifetime to the holy shrines in Mecca and Medina. He wears a seamless garment identical to those of all other pilgrims, and joins the multitude of pilgrims to review and renew his ties to the origins of his faith. Over the centuries since the Prophet's time, the pilgrimage has been one of the major unifying forces in Islam, the common bond that ties diverse believers from countries all over the globe into a single community.

Islam has much in common with Judaism and Christianity. Muhammad accepted Jewish revelations in the Torah (the first five books of the Old Testament), except for the covenant between God and the Hebrews or the special status of the Chosen People, and Christian revelations in the Gospels, excluding the divinity of Jesus and the idea of the Trinity. Muhammad regarded Jesus as simply one in a long line of God's prophets, beginning with Adam, moving through Abraham and Moses, including Jesus, and ending with Muhammad as the final voice for God's divine revelation and the Koran as the perfected vehicle for its transmission. "Before this book there was Moses' book . . . and this book confirms it in the Arabic tongue" (Koran 46:12).

The ten commandments are in the Koran, although the second, third, and fourth are worded differently. Muhammad borrowed numerous prohibitions from Judaism: pork is taboo, usury and gambling are forbidden, alcohol and blood are not to be consumed, idolatry is unpardonable, waste and pride are condemned.

Many of the Koran's instructions were aimed at ameliorating some of the social injustices that existed in Muhammad's time. Slavery is permitted under certain conditions, although the Koran urges that slaves be freed. Faith, patience, kindness, honesty, industry, honor, courage, and generosity are emphasized as desirable virtues. Other beliefs include a general resurrection, a final judgment of all mankind by God, eternal life in the hereafter, and God's knowledge of every man's acts and ultimate fate.

Islam presented a new religious law (the *shariah*), paralleling the older Jewish religious law, which was to regulate not only legal decisions, but also basic beliefs, religious practices, and social behavior. This law was to put an end to the incessant conflict between the tribes and their preoccupation with genealogical status by eliminating all previous distinctions and judging a man only according to the degree of his faith. "Oh mankind! We have created you man and woman, and have made you into nations and tribes that you may know each other. Verily, the noblest of you, in the sight of God, is he who is most God-fearing" (Koran 49:13). Because Moslem law is religious, its study becomes a form of worship, and the man who knows and understands *shariah* automatically possesses decisive authority and prestige.

There are over 600 million Moslems around the world today, and the numbers are growing, probably because of the universal appeal of the principle of brotherhood and equality of all men in the eyes of God. The largest Moslem communities are in the Middle East, North Africa, Indonesia, Malaysia, Bangladesh, and Pakistan. Moslem minorities live in all the countries of Africa bordering the southern edge of the Sa-

Kindergarten children being taught to pray in Kuwayt.

hara, on the east coast of Africa, in the southern Philippines, in central Russia, and in Europe in Turkey, Albania, and Yugoslavia.

Although the annual pilgrimage has brought many of them together, Moslems have never until recently had any sort of organized liaison. In 1965 King Faysal of Saudi Arabia launched in Mecca a ten-day international conference of Islamic nations, which met with enthusiastic response from both the Arab states and the non-Arab Moslems of Africa and Asia. By 1970 a Secretariat-General of this Moslem World League (or Islamic Conference, as it is often called in Western newspapers) was established in Jiddah, devoted to promoting the interests of the Moslem world and combatting Communism and Zionism. (Israel is regarded as an enemy of Islam as long as she occupies both Jerusalem, the third holiest city to Moslems after Mecca and Medina, and surrounding Arab lands.)

The annual conferences held in different Moslem nations have met with enthusiastic participation by many of their leading Moslem statesmen and thinkers, and specific measures have been taken to solve pressing current problems. At the 1975 conference, for example, the Arabs and Iranians agreed to continue a dialogue over all issues in the Gulf region as being in the best interest of all parties concerned. Also in 1975 an Islamic Development Bank was launched with a capital of over $2 billion subscribed by member states.

5

Language

No one knows how long the Arabic language has been spoken, but the Arabian Peninsula is certainly its homeland. The remarkable aspect of its origin is that Arabic evolved very early into a splendid poetic idiom among a nomadic pastoral people who were both illiterate and sparsely dispersed over an enormous geographical region. Because the Peninsula Arabs were nomadic, language was perhaps all that they had to utilize for intellectual stimulation and entertainment. In any case, the Arabs had developed their language into a remarkably complex vehicle for the expression of their pride and beliefs long before the birth of the Moslem religion.

In the Prophet Muhammad's time the poet was the historian and spokesman of his tribe. Because he knew the tribal lore and traditions, and expressed in his poetry the ideal manly characteristics of gallantry, courage, loyalty, independence, honesty, and generosity, he had the power to both inspire and sustain his people. Arabic tribal poetry developed a wealth of vocabulary and an opulent imagery that were the fountainhead of classical Arabic.

This poetic heritage, copied in the Koran, was diffused around the world by the spread of Islam. Written Arabic was not common before Muhammad's time, but the inspired style of the Koran has provided the model for all subsequent Arabic literature.

The authoritative version of the Koran was recorded in 651 A.D. Much of the Koran's impact, particularly when it is chanted, lies in the cadence and rhetoric of the language, which is lost when it is translated out of Arabic. The style is sonorous and rhythmic, and although it is not poetry, it is expressed in the unmetered verse or rhymed prose of traditional Arabic tribal poetry.

Beginning in the seventh century, the Moslem Arabs of the Peninsula carried their language to the many lands they conquered, where it was learned by all the neighboring peoples who originally spoke Semitic languages. The Moslem Empire did not endure, but the Arabic language is still spoken today by about 130 million people spread over 4.5 million square miles of the Middle East and Africa. Its alphabet is second only to the Latin alphabet in the extent of its usage. Even in countries with local languages completely different from Arabic, the scriptures of the Moslem religion, contained in the Koran and in the sayings of the Prophet Muhammad, are learned in the Arabic language (whether understood or not) wherever Islam is practiced. The one-sixth of the entire human race which professes the Moslem religion venerates Arabic as a language of special power and beauty.

For the Arabs themselves their language has a strong emotional appeal which touches and moves them in much the same way music does. At family celebrations and at gatherings during religious holidays, trained reciters read Koranic passages and formal, traditional poems describing the life of the Prophet, which are received with rapt attention. Such readings are common on the radio. Indeed, King Abdul Aziz ibn Saud justified the introduction of radio in Mecca in the 1920s as a vehicle for widespread transmission of the Koran. Arabs generally admire individuals who can recite from memory long sections of the Koran, and memorizing it was the major activity of the traditional religious schools connected with the local mosques.

Professional bards are still popular everywhere, especially during Ramadan, the Moslem month of fasting. They may ac-

A Saudi Arab boy reading the Koran.

company themselves instrumentally as they sing the folklore of the Arab past. They compose and sing new poems for wedding feasts and other rites of passage, and new epics are produced for the installation of a king or important shaykh, or to mark his passing. Laborers sing work songs while winnowing grain, pitting dates, riding camels, herding goats, loading cargo, trimming sail on ships, even while driving bulldozers or manning oil rigs. Many casual singers accompany themselves, either on traditional lute, zither, drum, tambourine, or one-string fiddle, or with that versatile adaptation from the New World which has a name of Arab origin, the guitar.

Spoken Arabic includes a number of separate and distinct regional dialects, not necessarily understood from region to region, but the written language known as classical Arabic—the polished language of the Koran—is used universally by all literate Arabic-speaking peoples. The ability to speak in formal Arabic is considered a mark of considerable erudition, not shared by or even comprehensible to the ordinary citizen.

The exceptionally high value that Arabs put on their language causes them to overassert, to exaggerate, and to repeat far more than English-speakers, for example. This leads to confusion on both sides when foreigners take what Arabs say at face value, while Arabs are not convinced of the validity of simple assertions in English. Arabs use verbal threats to relieve tension and vent hostility far more often than Westerners do. This is a device which substitutes words for action, although it may not be recognized as such by outsiders.

Another source of great confusion for Westerners in understanding Arabs is that Arabic verb tenses do not correspond to ours. Nor is the Arab's sense of history stretched out on a time line; rather, it is focused on the occurrence of clusters of important events. The tendency to overstate any case to the point where it seems exaggerated to non-Arabs, combined with the lack of precision as to the relationship of specific events to the other activities that are part of man's behavior, makes accurate understanding and communication between Arabs and non-Arabs very tricky.

Arabic is a Semitic language, one of a group of ancient languages of which only Arabic and Hebrew are widely spoken today. Like Hebrew, Arabic is written from right to left on the page in an artistically flowing cursive script. The Arabic alphabet, developed originally and streamlined by the Phoenicians, has twenty-eight letters, all representing consonants. Vowels can be indicated by marks above and below the letters, although these are ordinarily omitted.

The transliteration of Arabic into English is very difficult because the Arabic alphabet contains letters which the English does not, as well as sounds for which there are no English equivalents. The letter ʿain, for example, is usually represented by ʿ and signifies a minute pause with a catch in the breath. The word *Saudi* in Saudi Arabia, for example, should have an ʿain between the *a* and the *u*, so that it is spoken in syllables.

The other really difficult letter is *ghain*, often written in English as *q* or *gh*, but actually a soft guttural sound, much like clearing a feather from the back of the mouth. The name of the country which is spelled Qatar actually sounds more like "gutter," with a gentle rasping in the throat at the beginning.

Arabic names of places and people often seem very confusing to the non-Arabic speaker, but much of this difficulty arises from the transliteration of Arabic words into the English alphabet. The Red Sea port of Jiddah, for example, is also commonly spelled Jeddah or Juddah. This happens because the unstressed vowel sound that linguists call *schwa* can be indicated in English by several different vowels. The fault is with English spellings, not with Arabic. For the most part words in this book use the Library of Congress system of transliteration without the macrons and subscript dots which indicate vowels and non-English letters. A few exceptions have been made for very common names such as Abu Dhabi (rather than Abu Zabi) and Sharjah (rather than Sharqah). Alternate spellings are given for names that are not commonly spelled as the Library of Congress does, such as Kuwayt, which is more usually written Kuweit, and Bahrayn, more usually Bahrein. In pronouncing Arabic words, all *a*'s should sound as though they have an *h* after them, unless they have a *y* after them to indicate a long *a* as in "late."

In Arabic, like French, all nouns have gender, and the article "the" precedes them. In Arabic "the" is *al* (or *el*), and this prefix appears commonly in place names, such as Al Madinah (Medina), and in family names, such as the Al Saud family, where it is used to indicate a distinguished lineage. A number of common English words which have come directly from Arabic retain the *al:* albatross, alcohol, alfalfa, algebra, and alkali are examples.

One of the favorite examples used to show the richness and diversity of the Arabic language is the many variations in the word for "camel"—as many as a thousand. There is no single word that identifies camels as such. Instead there are different words in both singular and plural which specify the breed, the color, the purpose (riding camels are different from herd camels), the animal's sex, its age in each year of its life until it is fully grown and when it begins to grow old, and so on. There are special words for female camels that have not borne calves, that are about to bear calves, that have recently borne calves and are still nursing them. Perhaps no other word in

Arabic has so many different forms, unless it is the many terms for "sword."

Sometime before 800 A.D. the Arabs adopted the Indian system of using smaller clusters of written number symbols than the Latin, thus greatly simplifying written computations. The numerals themselves are probably based on the Arabic alphabet, and the Arabs introduced the concept of zero to indicate a unitary value of nothing. (The Arabic *sifr,* cipher in English, means "empty.") Their numerals were carried to Spain about 900, and transmitted thence to the rest of Europe after 1100. The ten basic symbols—0 through 9—in which all numbers can be expressed were so much simpler than any others in use that Arabic numerals became the most commonly used throughout the world.

6

Customs

Patterns of life throughout the Arabian Peninsula today, as in centuries past, are shaped by Bedouin heritage, Moslem religion, and the Arabs' great love of their language. The Peninsula Arab still maintains his close ties with and membership in his extended family and his egalitarian attitude toward his fellow man. He shakes hands with everyone he meets, regardless of rank, and the lowliest employee sits down comfortably with his employer to chat, drink tea, or share a meal. He is probably devout in observing the practices of his religious faith, and invokes God's name in almost every statement he makes because he believes that his whole destiny is already known by God.

The traditional patterns of thought are deeply ingrained, but frequently they come into conflict with the requirements of a modernizing economy financed by petroleum and cause the educated Arab to feel a certain amount of ambivalence toward his own culture. He admires Western technology and ideas, but cherishes his own Arab heritage and finds it difficult to slough off age-old attitudes. For example, the belief that everything that happens is predestined would seem to make it unnecessary to be provident or plan far ahead, yet no country can invest billions of petrodollars without a great deal of careful advance planning. The Arab's attitude toward work is an inheritance from his Bedouin ancestors, who regarded tending flocks of animals and raiding as the only honorable professions and menial labor as demeaning activity. This attitude causes today's Arab to prefer to leave menial tasks to foreign workers. The Arabs put great store by self-respect, which derives from the great stress the Bedouin placed on personal honor. Self-respect is thus based on the attitude of others toward oneself, and the Arabs feel compelled to direct their activities so as to maintain face in public, which often conflicts with efficiency or rapid accomplishment of specific goals.

Such attitudes are contrary to the requirements of a modern money economy and will gradually be modified as more and more Arabs become involved in managerial and technological activities and the many services that support those activities. However, it is important to know the customs and traditions that have shaped the attitudes of the Arabs in order to understand what kinds of difficulties they face in adjusting to their changing situation.

Family ties determine the structure of society throughout the Arabian Peninsula, an inheritance from the days when the nomadic clan was the basic social and economic unit in a hostile desert environment. Close-knit families, working together to tend their flocks and move them from pasture to pasture, were essential to survival. Coupled with the organization of society on kinship lines is the long-accepted regulation of family, clan, and tribal life by Moslem law, so that a strong ethical basis strengthens family and kin affiliations and mutual obligations.

The Arab family is not just father, mother, and children. Its nucleus is generally all the brothers of one generation, their

Schoolchildren in Abu Dhabi.

wives and children, grandparents if they still survive, possibly some elderly aunts and uncles, and maybe some cousins who have no family to care for them. That is, these family units are organized around closely related males, with descent traced in the father's side of the family. It is this family unit which is the source of identity for each individual in it. Family obligations come before all others.

An Arab family lives together. If they are nomadic herdsmen, their home is a cluster of tents set up beside a well or spring. If they are settled farmers, their home is a series of interconnected rooms which face away from the street onto a central courtyard. City dwellers may enjoy a house or apart-

An old town in central Saudi Arabia.

ment which houses only part of an extended family, but even these maintain close ties with their kin in the village from which they originally came.

City dwellers also continue many of the customs of their Bedouin ancestors, such as having separate living rooms where men and women socialize apart from each other. Cushions and bolsters on the floor of such living rooms replicate the atmosphere of hospitality and informality of the desert tent. The beautiful Persian carpets that serve as furniture and sleeping mats in the Bedouin's tents now grace the floors of apartments, villas, and sun-dried block dwellings. Every guest is still made to feel immediately at ease as he joins the relaxed family circle sitting on cushions on the floor. It's impossible to feel stiff or formal when sitting this way. Much warmth and swift acceptance of outsiders will be lost if the Arabs decide to adopt Western-style furniture, for its use will inevitably make social contacts more formal and diminish the delightful assimilation of guests into an easy fellowship that Arab families now enjoy.

The open warmth of the Peninsula Arabs also derives from their nomadic background. In a harsh desert landscape the traveler on the move is very apt to be dependent on the next man he meets for some essential to his existence—food, water, shelter, or transport. Such interdependence breeds immediate acceptance and a willingness to reveal frankly who you are, where you came from, where you are going, and what news you picked up along the way. The same kind of quick acceptance and concern for one's fellow men characterized the frontier society of the American West, where the services one extended to a stranger were reciprocated by the next man, and the willingness to lend a helping hand was often crucial to the stranger's progress.

The Arabs of the Peninsula carry this concept of hospitality even further and consider it their duty to make a guest welcome, offer him sustenance, and safeguard his person. Even an enemy, if he can reach tent shelter, must be protected for at least three days, because no man could survive in the desert by cunning alone, but required food and water to give him a chance of eluding pursuers. Thus a man in flight can seek respite in the camp of his enemies; a woman can put herself into the hands of strangers; and a traveler can leave his possessions with people he has never seen before. All feel honor bound to care for the stranger's needs as though they were his own.

The next larger kinship circle is the clan, composed of several extended families who are related to one another by descent from a common male ancestor several generations earlier. Related clans which recognize ties to each other consider themselves part of a larger kin unit, the tribe. Some tribes are very small, consisting of only a few clans; others are very large, and enjoy considerable power and prestige. No matter how nebulous his ancestry may be or how far removed he is from tribal life, almost every Peninsula Arab can tell you what tribe he belongs to, and the fact of belonging is to him a source of pride and an obligation to aid his fellow tribesmen.

Among the nomadic herdsmen, of course, the tribal structure remains intact today, for related clans still move together seeking grasslands for their animals, and pitch their tent camps in clusters near a water source during the dry season. Each clan is headed by a shaykh, chosen usually from a particular family which has the hereditary right to lead the clan. The individual whom the male heads of the families in the clan agree should be their leader is, however, the person whom they trust and believe has leadership qualities, and he serves by their consent and can be replaced if he fails to live up to their expectations. The shaykh consults with the other clan elders, and based on their advice makes decisions for the whole clan, settles disputes, and represents the tribe in relations with other tribes and with the central government. A combination of clans into a tribe will be headed by one tribal chief—a shaykh who is the consensus choice of all the clan leaders. The shaykh holds regular *majlis* (a council of family heads and clan spokesmen) where he conducts tribal business and hears complaints. Before modern governments were instituted, a traditional shaykh or *amir* (another title for a tribal leader) and his male relatives were expected to protect the community and maintain Moslem law, while the ruler expected his subjects to obey his decisions and to mobilize occasionally to combat a crisis.

Village organization also is based on kinship ties. Small villages consist of one related clan, living close together, tending fields and herds cooperatively, perhaps exchanging animal products with nomads who come regularly to the village to trade for staple foods and manufactured items needed in the desert. A village headman will be chosen from a leading family, and he too will meet regularly with the men of the village in open council to manage village affairs and assign community duties. The village will have a public well, a mosque, a marketplace (*suq*), some small shops, probably a government school and a clinic, perhaps a cafe where men may spend their leisure time drinking tea or coffee together.

In larger villages several related clans will be grouped together, each unit living in dwellings placed close together, perhaps giving their name to that particular section of the village. In addition to the village headman and the imam (religious leader) of the mosque, there will probably be a *qadi* (religious judge) who hears cases involving interpretation of the *shariah*. The headman will hold an appointment from the central government, for today he is part of a national administration which makes him responsible to the *amir* in the next higher administrative unit in his region.

Modern economic activities have prompted the settlement of new villages where unrelated kin groups may be found living together, as around pump stations along the oil pipeline that carries petroleum from the Gulf to the Mediterranean, or in agricultural development schemes, or in workers' towns in the oil fields. Here economic activity plays a much larger role in giving residents their identity and status than is the rule in the traditional settlements of the Peninsula.

Larger towns, of course, consist of many unrelated kin groups, but here again the extended family is still the fundamental organization unit of society, and relations are maintained within larger kin groups or well-known or powerful tribal groups. A town will have a small group of prominent families of high status who are involved in governing and religious activities as well as in the direction of workers involved in the economic, manufacturing, trading, and commercial activities of the community. The towns are linked to the central administration by the appointment of officials from the prominent families who are responsible for smaller village units in their region, and are in turn responsible to higher officials in the central government structure.

A town will have its public wells, marketplace, shops, cafes, mosque, clinic, and government school. It will probably also have police and fire posts, playgrounds, and perhaps a youth center and a public library. Clubs or community gathering places are generally lacking, however, for joining organizations is not an Arab custom. Social life is generally carried on within the home, particularly for women. Television has rapidly become a favorite family pastime, and music, theater, and private film showings are becoming occasional sources of entertainment in the larger towns. Festival occasions are celebrated with a great deal of enthusiasm—weddings, circumcisions, birthdays, and religious holidays—and include feasting, group dancing, oral recitations, and musical renditions of epic ballads. Two important religious holidays receive the most attention—Id al-Adha, which is the feast of sacrifice during the pilgrimage, and Id al Fitr, the feast at the breaking of the fast at the end of Ramadan. Sporting events such as soccer and horseracing are popular among the men. Wealthy Arabs enjoy hunting with falcons, yachting on the coasts, and owning and racing the small, fast Arabian horse, which is a status symbol in this part of the world.

Arabs' participation in community organizations is minimal because their associations are based on kinship relations. Social activities are family activities, and leisure and entertainment are not valued for themselves but as an integral part of family routine. Because of a strong tradition of mutual obligations among families, business arrangements are apt to be organized on a family basis as well. Urban business concerns generally include father, sons and brothers, or uncles and nephews working together. Nomadic encampments and farming villages are generally self-sustaining economic units, with land grazed or tilled in common by a large family unit. Every individual is expected to give assistance to related family members whenever the opportunity arises. Younger people are expected to take care of their elders and to enjoy doing so. This kind of ingroup support may not always be efficient, but it does provide all family members with a large degree of security.

In the present era most Moslem marriages are monoga-

Falconry is a very popular sport among upper-class Arab men.

mous, although some men have more than one wife when they can afford to provide separate quarters for each and treat each equally. A wife leaves her family to live with her husband's kin, but maintains ties to her own parents, and her personal conduct continues to reflect on her father's reputation. In order to maintain family status, or to keep bloodlines pure, or to preserve family property intact, marriages are often arranged within the kin group, preferably between children of brothers or other male relatives.

Marriage is regarded as a civil contract, and is usually arranged by the parents. The prospective husband makes a bridal payment to the girl's father, which is used to buy jewelry, clothing, articles for her prospective home, or livestock or other property which will serve as an investment for her future security. It may help defray the expenses of the wedding festivities. A man who is divorced or deserted by his wife may demand the return of his bridal payment, which is strong incentive for families to try to persuade their daughters to stay with their husbands.

Often marriage ties are of great political importance, both in cementing alliances between clans and in the gathering of important information that is not available to men in their public roles. The wives of senior members of ruling families are often the route through which many members of the community approach the shaykhs. Shaykhah Hussah, wife of a recent ruler of Dubay, was so highly esteemed that she held her own public audiences for both men and women visitors who sought her advice and help. Her husband, Shaykh Said ibn Maktum, reduced himself to penury in a political struggle in 1939 and 1940, and it was his wife's canny business sense that restored the family fortunes. This is an unusual example of liberation in a traditional society.

Probably no area of Moslem custom is more surprising to outsiders than the status of women and their subservient relationship to their husbands. The Arabian Peninsula is still a male-oriented and -dominated society, and most Arab women there are trained from childhood to be wives and mothers and to center their activities in the home. The Arab husband is expected to make decisions for his family in all activities and obligations outside the home, but the wife is in charge of the household and is responsible for children, daughters-in-law, servants, and even the men themselves as far as household routine is concerned.

Arranged marriages might seem to ignore personal feelings, but they tend to work out well, since marriage partners are usually closely related or at least share very similar backgrounds. Well-educated Arabs will tell you that because Arab boys and girls are taught to respect each other, their marriages develop greater harmony and lasting affection than those based on passionate romantic attachments. Kindness and consideration are highly esteemed virtues in relations between husband and wife. Because Arabian men and women have traditionally found companionship and intellectual stimulation among members of the same sex, they have not sought these qualities in marriage partners. This situation is changing as more and more young Arab men and women receive university educations, particularly overseas.

Marriages used to occur while bride and groom were between sixteen and eighteen, but lengthened education and higher bride payments are tending to delay the marrying age. However, bachelors and spinsters are very rare; everyone is expected to get married.

Marriage is intended to be permanent, but divorce is not uncommon and carries no disgrace. However, interfamily pressures act as a fairly strong deterrent to divorce, since husband and wife are usually closely related. The most usual causes are incompatibility, barrenness, and lack of support.

The procedure for the husband is very simple and requires only a declaration of his intention to divorce his wife. He is expected to provide a short period of support for her and to take care of his young children, who generally stay with their mother until age twelve. It is more difficult for a woman to obtain a divorce, and pressure from her family to carry on is considerably greater, but a woman can seek to end her marriage through the office of a *qadi*. Mistreatment, lack of support, desertion, or failure to obtain her consent before taking another wife are sufficient grounds.

Islamic law strictly regulates inheritance. Men receive about double the share of women, because women receive substantial dowries when they marry and are supported by their husbands.

Children live and play together until they are about seven or eight. After that boys are expected to spend more time in the company of their fathers, while girls move into the female circle and participate in the domestic activities of the household. Education is segregated by sex at all ages, even at the university level where closed circuit television brings male lecturers to women students.

Family customs are, of course, changing in the Arabian Peninsula as the oil industry and government development plans open up new avenues for making a living and achieving status. Salaried jobs greatly decrease economic dependence on family ties, and modern education transforms aspirations. The most conspicuous evidence of change is the movement from nomadic tents and mud-brick dwellings to modern villas and apartments. Rising revenues have made possible an enormous amount of construction, and urban Arabs are becoming accustomed to using modern urban services—electricity, piped fresh water, sewage systems, radio and television, personal au-

A game of netball at a school in Bahrayn.

tomobiles, multiple appliances, buses, supermarkets, and neighborhood schools.

Providing new housing for all those who want it presents problems, however, for construction does not keep pace with demand from local residents, and an enormous influx of foreigners coming to the Peninsula to work in an endless array of new activities also requires housing. A common complaint expressed today is that rents have been driven out of sight by foreign businesses which will pay any price in order to secure accommodations for their employees. This makes it very difficult for the less affluent Arab who would also like to move up to pleasanter quarters. Real estate also offers the opportunity to make a fortune far more easily than plodding away at a government appointment or grubbing to establish a business, yet contributes far less to a stable economy. Hotel space particularly is at a premium, and extremely difficult to find. Even though tourism is not yet encouraged in the Peninsula, the new luxury hotels that have been built in the last decade or two are always booked full with foreign businessmen who have come to sell their wares, and the room rates are as high as those in New York or London.

Along with an eagerness to adopt the comforts of modern housing has come a taste for imported goods—not only automobiles, refrigerators, radios, and televisions, but also foods and beverages from all over the world. In isolated rural areas, of course, such goodies are not so readily available, and diets will continue to be predominantly traditional: roast mutton served on heaps of rice with side dishes of roasted or fried eggplant, mixed green salads, eggs and cheese, topped off with fruit or custard with raisins and almonds for dessert.

Outdoor clothing continues traditional, even in the cities. Although Arabs who have come to the Peninsula from other Arab countries wear European-style clothing, local men still dress in the ankle-length white shirt called a *thobe* (*thawb*) and the large square head scarf called a *gutra*, held in place by a black or white cord called an *agal* (*aigal, iqal*). This costume is practical for hot, dry climates, for the *thobe* is loose and lets air circulate while it shields the skin from the burning sun, and the *gutra* shelters the head and keeps out both heat and blowing sand. Over the *thobe* in cooler weather is worn a long white flowing robe called *dishdashah* or a heavy woolen outer cloak called *aba*. This costume is identical for all Arabian men, except that Bedouin or their descendants prefer the red-and-white checked *gutra*, while townsmen choose a plain white head covering. There are few clues in clothing to indicate an individual's economic status or social position, except for the gold *agal* and gold cording of the ruling family. Costumes in Yemen and Oman differ slightly from those elsewhere in the Peninsula, particularly in the headcloth worn turban style by the men.

Tribeswomen in Yemen wear trousers and are not veiled. Elsewhere in the Peninsula women still wear a long black outer cloak (*abbayah*) over their garments when they are on the street or in public places, with a black chiffon veil over their faces. Like that of the men, this public garment gives no clue to economic status or social position. However, under the *abbayah* may be anything from the most elegant Paris fashions to blue jeans. Modesty requires that legs and arms be covered.

The *abbayah* is the garment that attracts the attention of foreigners, who are startled by the idea of hiding all women from public view. This kind of seclusion is based on centuries of custom and has its origin in the heavy stress laid on family honor. *Purdah* (seclusion) was given sanction by Islam as a means of keeping women pure and out of reach of the baser appetites of society.

The fact that Peninsula women are still wearing the *abbayah* gives the impression that they are still in seclusion, completely cut off from contact with any men other than the members of their extended families. This is the case among conservative and traditional families. However, among families who have become involved in the activities of the outside world, the women, although they still wear their *abbayahs* on the street, are now mixing socially with their husbands' friends, business associates, and casual acquaintances in the same way that Western women do. Schooling for women was started in Saudi Arabia in 1960, in Bahrayn and Aden before that, in Kuwayt and the other oil shaykhdoms a little later. The first generation of educated women is finding its place in society, many of

A young woman of Qatar.

them going on to university, and they are mixing freely within their homes with a wide variety of male acquaintances whom they would not have been able to meet twenty-five years ago. They are as poised, outgoing, and stimulating as educated women anywhere in the world.

Several dozen young women are working for the Arabian American Oil Company, side by side with their male colleagues, and are pioneers who are breaking ground for their sisters and cousins who will follow their example. In the past women have been tutored at home and have engaged in activities like teaching and nursing where they deal only with other women, but in fields like these too the example of many non-veiled women from other Arab countries who have migrated to the Peninsula to meet job demands encourages local women to expand the circle of their own activities.

If you ask a young Saudi woman with a university degree and a career of her own why she still wears the *abbayah*, she will tell you that it avoids unpleasant incidents on the street, and that is the only place she wears it. Some young women are taking the preliminary step of reducing the thickness of their chiffon veil from three layers to only one, which can be seen through, or of omitting the veil altogether.

No one seems quite certain when the *abbayah* will be discarded, except that it will probably be a very gradual thing. The women of the Peninsula do not expect that a custom as deeply established as this will be abolished by royal decree, although royal decrees in more minor areas certainly contribute to a general trend to reduce the restrictions on the lives of women. The establishment of schools for girls was a major step. A recent royal decree has ordered that every Saudi woman have her photo in her passport, which not only countermands the Moslem prohibition against representation of the human image, but also sends the woman to a public photography studio where an unrelated male will take her picture. There is also a lot of speculation over mounting pressure to permit women to drive, which would release male drivers for other urgent needs and would certainly require abandonment of the veil. Other critical manpower shortages will work toward permitting the female half of the adult population to enter public employment. Small steps already taken include employment of women in the offices of the new Intercontinental Hotel in Riyadh and in government television.

In other Moslem countries like Pakistan, the emancipation of women from *purdah* has taken only a short quarter century—the time span required for a generation of educated women to move into public roles. Even there, some conservative women still prefer to observe the ancient custom. The women of the Arabian Peninsula will probably follow much the same gradual change in their living patterns, moving gracefully into the niches which their rapidly changing society opens up for them.

7

Nationhood

Tribal traditions and loyalty to strong leaders have led to the emergence of eight separate political units on the Arabian Peninsula. Some sort of federation of several or all of these nations would be far more efficient economically, but would receive little popular support. Saudi Arabia is the geographical giant of the group because the Al Saud clan struggled for over a century to achieve dominion over their neighbors in central Arabia, and succeeded finally under the outstanding leadership of King Abdul Aziz ibn Saud.

Equally proud chieftains have established shaykhdoms along the coasts, and their tribesmen have given allegiance to their rulers rather than to an area of land or to the abstract concept of nationhood. This ancient tribal loyalty has fragmented the map of Arabia from time immemorial, and will probably continue to do so until an entire generation of citizens has been educated and involved in the modern money economy.

Yemen and Oman, the countries of the Arabian Peninsula about which we know the least, have the longest histories. Yemen was ruled until 1962 (except for interruptions by the Turks) by a line of Shia imams of the Zaydi sect of Islam who moved with their followers from Iraq in the ninth century and took control of Yemen. The Sultans of Oman have been autonomous rulers since 1650, except for a brief period of Persian rule. Leaders in both these countries preferred in the twentieth century to avoid contact with the outside world and actively cultivated an isolation which kept foreigners away and prevented the introduction of foreign ideas into their societies.

Oman. The Sultans of Oman ruled under British protection from 1789 until 1951, when Britain recognized Oman as a fully autonomous state. Even after that, British support of the Sultan of Oman was necessary in 1963 against the Moslem religious leader of Oman (an imam of the Ibadi reform sect which had dominated Omani religious life since the ninth century), who claimed that he controlled an autonomous state. British encouragement of a United Nations investigation resulted in the Imam's exile.

Sultan Sayid Qabus (Qaboos) ibn Said Al Bu Said deposed his father in 1970 because the father was reluctant to spend oil revenues on development. He wanted to maintain Oman's traditional isolation, keeping out both foreigners and their ideas. He imposed restrictions against all mechanical conveyances, newspapers, music, smoking, and foreign trinkets such as sunglasses, flashlights, cameras, and umbrellas.

Sultan Qabus, the fourteenth sovereign in his dynasty, was educated at Sandhurst in England and has no such fears of Western ideas. He has energetically undertaken a major development program in an attempt to bring his country rapidly into the twentieth century. This has considerably enhanced his reputation among his people, but has also spurred rapidly rising expectations which may cost more than Oman can afford, particularly since half the country's income is being eaten up by defense.

High military expenditures have been necessitated by a Marxist-oriented separatist movement in Dhofar Province in western Oman, directed by a revolutionary group based in Aden in Southern Yemen, and armed by the Soviet Union. Its aim is to overthrow all traditional rulers along the Gulf, particularly Sultan Qabus, who still relies on British advisers, contract consultants, and military personnel to provide a large proportion of Oman's high-level manpower.

The Yemen Arab Republic. The long religious rule of the Zaydi imams in Yemen ended in 1962 when the very unpopular Imam Ahmad was succeeded by his son Badr. The army rebelled, destroyed the palace, gained control of Sana and the other main towns, and established the Yemen Arab Republic. Yemeni military leaders asked the United Arab Republic (Egypt) for troops and supplies to fight the deposed Imam, whose royalist forces were aided by Jordan and Saudi Arabia, with whom the Imam had joint defense agreements.

Although Egypt and Saudi Arabia made several abortive attempts to extricate themselves from the conflict, intermittent fighting went on until the 1967 Arab-Israeli War. Then, at an Arab summit conference, King Faysal of Saudi Arabia and President Nasser of Egypt agreed to terminate their role in the hostilities in Yemen. Recently Saudi Arabia has begun supplying arms to Yemen to replace those earlier supplied by Russia.

The government of the Yemen Arab Republic is largely military. Control is in the hands of a seven-man Command Council (of which the chairman is chief of state), aided by a prime minister and cabinet appointed by the council. A constitution was adopted in 1971 and nation-wide elections chose a 159-member assembly. However, the constitution was temporarily suspended in 1974 and a somewhat modified form of government adopted which strengthened the rule of the Command Council.

Saudi Arabia. The giant of the Arabian Peninsula, Saudi Arabia, occupies four-fifths of its total area. Unification of the many tribes of central Arabia into one state began in the early part of the eighteenth century when the Al Saud family of Diriyah, a town south of Riyadh, became the staunch supporters of the Wahhabi reform movement to purify Islam. The Al Saud chiefs fought, with varying degrees of success, over the next two centuries to unite the interior tribes of the Peninsula and free them from Turkish rule.

The goal was finally achieved by Abdul Aziz ibn Saud, who emerged at age twenty from exile in Kuwayt to capture Riyadh in 1902 and make it his capital. Over the next quarter century he maneuvered and rallied the tribes to his banners, first to fight the Turks in the west, then the Rashidis of northern Arabia, then the Turks in the eastern Al Hasa Oasis.

World War I ended Ottoman Turkish rule in the Arabian Peninsula. The British controlled Aden and had treaty arrangements with all the shaykhs on the Arabian coast of the Gulf. In order to end Ottoman control of his country, Abdul Aziz concluded a similar treaty with the British in 1915, which recognized his control over much of Arabia and guaranteed British protection of his sovereignty.

The northern borders of Saudi Arabia were established in the 1920s through treaties negotiated with the British, representing the interests of Jordan, Iraq, and Kuwayt. Neutral zones were established in two places, one between Iraq and Saudi Arabia and the other between Kuwayt and Saudi Arabia, to permit the traditional movement of tribes roaming the region in search of pasture and water.

However, the Hijaz, that important mountain area of western Arabia where Mecca and Medina are located, remained in the hands of the rival Hashemite family, supported by the British. Abdul Aziz ibn Saud and his Wahhabi-inspired army moved against Hijaz in 1924 and defeated the Hashemite defenders.

In 1927 the protection treaty with Britain was ended. Pacification of the interior of Arabia took several more years, until in 1932 Abdul Aziz ibn Saud became king of a united Saudi Arabia. He immediately opened the eastern part of his country to oil exploration, which led to the discovery of oil in commercial quantities in 1938. Large-scale production followed World War II.

Abdul Aziz ibn Saud died in 1953 and was succeeded first by his eldest son Saud, then by Saud's younger brother Faysal. King Faysal presided over ten years of tremendous expansion and development in Saudi Arabia, and set in motion the First Five Year Development Plan which provided for a modern education system and health services, a greatly expanded transportation and communications network, measures to improve the agricultural potential of the country, and the beginnings of modern local industry. He encouraged the continuing settlement of the Bedouin, improvement in the status of women through provision of schools for girls, and greater individual freedom through updated codified law.

Faysal continued the traditional Bedouin custom of being accessible to his people, and held regular audiences where any of his countrymen could bring petitions to him personally.

Unfortunately, in 1975 a nephew took advantage of his accessibility and assassinated him during a royal audience.

The royal family and the *ulama* (council of religious leaders) immediately exercised their prerogative and put his brother, Crown Prince Khalid, oldest of ibn Saud's surviving sons, on the throne. The next in line, Prince Fahd, was appointed Crown Prince, Deputy Prime Minister, and Minister of Interior.

The office of king in Saudi Arabia is not hereditary. He is chosen from among the royal princes of the Saud family, of whom there are three thousand or so, by responsible members of the royal family. The Saud family, which is part of the Anayzah tribe and includes several hundred closely related members and a wide circle of more distant relatives, has assumed the role of the dominant tribe in Saudi Arabia. It possesses both military strength and great wealth. There are no political parties and no franchise, so that political activity on a national scale is in the hands of the Saud clan and the important tribal shaykhs and other leading families, to all of whom the Sauds are related by marriage.

The king's power is very much a result of his personal style and his ability to meet the needs of the time. King Abdul Aziz ibn Saud was a desert shaykh who possessed the military prowess and personal charisma to unite the fractious Arab tribes. His son King Saud tried unsuccessfully to continue the paternalistic rule of his father in an era of rapid change when

The late King Faysal of Saudi Arabia during a visit to oil installations in the early development days of the industry.

government was becoming increasingly complex. Faysal succeeded in achieving a delicate balance between preserving the traditional values of Islam and Arab society and helping his people adjust to a rapidly changing world. He believed in gradual evolution, and was equally at home with sophisticated foreigners and the desert Bedouin. His own modest and austere lifestyle set an example for those who were inclined to squander wealth on the material benefits it could buy. He also saw to it that those individuals who had learned Western ideas through education in the United States or Europe were moved quickly into important governmental, economic, or professional positions where their talents would be absorbed in national development rather than turned to political activity against the state.

King Khalid has continued Faysal's policies, committing the enormous oil revenues of his country to a massive plan to modernize its economy and society.

Kuwayt. In the coastal states of the Peninsula British influence continued until after the middle of the twentieth century. Kuwayt was under British treaty protection from 1899 until 1961, when its full independence was recognized. Iraq immediately announced its claim to Kuwayt, rejecting border agreements made with the British in 1922. British troops returned to Kuwayt to protect the new kingdom. This force was soon replaced by Arab troops from Saudi Arabia, Jordan, the United Arab Republic, and Sudan. In 1963 the Iraq government in Baghdad was overthrown, and the succeeding government muted its claim. Later Kuwayt and Iraq concluded a trade and economic agreement, but border tensions rose again in 1973 to brief armed clashes, and the question of Iraqi intentions is still unsettled.

Shaykh Abdullah, the eleventh consecutive ruler of Kuwayt

in the Al Sabah line, had assumed office in 1950 and continued traditional paternal rule. After independence, however, he chose to give his people a constitutional form of government. The constitution adopted in 1962 provides for a fifty-member National Assembly to share legislative power with the shaykh, its members elected by adult male suffrage for four-year terms. In 1976 political unrest among the large immigrant population led the shaykh to suspend the constitution. There are no political parties, but the formation of trade unions was authorized in 1964. A prime minister and council of ministers control fourteen government departments. The judicial system is based on traditional Moslem law, which has been codified for modern usage.

The first ruler of independent Kuwayt, Shaykh Abdullah, and his brother who succeeded him in 1965, Amir Shaykh Sabah Al Salim al Sabah, have guided their country from a traditional desert shaykhdom into a highly prosperous welfare state with a free economy. They chose two methods of distributing the enormous wealth that the sale of crude oil was channeling into their treasury. First, the government bought land to make room for steadily increasing government activities. These continual land purchases put wealth into the private hands of about half the shaykhdom's citizens. Second, the rulers have created a welfare system which includes the provision of income supplements to maintain a satisfactory level of living for all Kuwaytis.

Bahrayn. Farther south on the Gulf coast of the Arabian Peninsula Britain had treaty relationships with Bahrayn, Qatar, and the shaykhs of the Trucial Coast since early in the nineteenth century. In Bahrayn, oil revenues after 1932 permitted the development of a modern government administration as well as an educated and fairly skilled local labor force. Growing demands for popular representation in government in the 1950s led to strikes and unrest, which forced Shaykh Salman Al Khalifa to adopt emergency rule and put stern restrictions on dissent and political activity. He announced token measures to broaden the base of his government through an Administrative Council which would help conduct government affairs, but since its membership was largely from the royal family, paternal rule continued dominant.

Further serious labor disturbances occurred in 1965 and led to riots against the ruling family and the British. In 1968 Britain announced that she would end all her protective treaty arrangements in the Gulf in 1971. Attempts were made before British departure to federate Bahrayn, Qatar, and the Trucial Coast, but the idea foundered in the face of traditional tribal rivalries and distrust, disparities in wealth, population, education, and modern approach. Bahrayn and Qatar opted for independence separately, while the seven Trucial shaykhdoms joined together in a federation called the United Arab Amirates.

Bahrayn opted to experiment with parliamentary institutions. At the time of independence in 1971 Shaykh Isa ibn Salman Al Khalifa wielded almost absolute power, but in response to the growing political pressures of the 1950s and 1960s and serious unrest in the early 1970s, the ruler announced the appointment of a forty-one-member constituent assembly in 1972 to debate a draft constitution, which was adopted in 1973.

The new constitution contained a number of radical changes in the country's government. For one, it provided that the constitution, when adopted, could not be changed by anyone—electorate or ruler—for five years. It established a thirty-member elected National Assembly to be the principal law-making body. It guaranteed rights to women and to trade unions, and a voice to the National Assembly in granting concessions to exploit natural resources. Political parties are still prohibited, however, and the royal family continues to control the executive offices of government. Islam is the official religion and the *shariah* the basis of law.

Qatar. In Qatar the ruler signed a treaty of friendship with Britain immediately after independence in 1971 to replace the former treaty of protection. British officers direct the Qatar security forces and are prominent in the management of the Qatar Petroleum Company and Shell (Qatar), Ltd., which provide 95 percent of government revenues.

Qatar has an interim constitution adopted in 1970 as a Basic Law, which includes a bill of rights and provides a legal framework within which modern government can evolve. A fourteen-member cabinet led by a prime minister is appointed by the ruler to formulate public policy and direct the various ministries which carry on government activities.

In 1972, with the approval of the powerful Al Thani family, Shaykh Khalifa ibn Hamad Al Thani quietly deposed his autocratic and somewhat spendthrift cousin who was then ruler. Shaykh Khalifa became both ruler and prime minister, with a cabinet consisting primarily of members of the Al Thani family. Estimated to number twenty thousand people, this is the largest ruling family among the Gulf shaykhdoms. The Al Thani have managed to keep Qatar fairly serene so far, but the family is split into three main branches, and rivalry among the branches of the dynasty is a persistent problem. They work together to keep other clans from challenging their control of the country, and are providing a wide range of welfare benefits—housing, water, electricity, transport, health services, education, and the like. Qatar citizens pay no income taxes. Government sets up and runs enterprises to spur development in the commercial sector, then sells shares to private investors who are eventually to take them over.

United Arab Amirates. When treaty arrangements between Britain and the seven Trucial States ended in 1971, these shaykhdoms formed a federation. The seven amirates vary greatly in population and wealth, for three of them are pumping and exporting oil, while the others have almost no resources whatsoever. The federation itself is minuscule compared with its neighbors of the Arabian Peninsula. All the people are concentrated in the settlements that give the amirates their separate names—Abu Dhabi, Dubay, Sharjah, Ras al Khaymah, Umm al Qaywayn, Ajman, and Fujayrah—with only a scattered Bedouin population inhabiting the barren stretches away from the sea where there is almost no ground water and hardly any rain.

The interior gives way to the desolate sands of the Empty Quarter of Saudi Arabia, and no defined boundary separates the two countries. Nothing exists there to disagree over except the Al Buraymi (Buraimi) Oasis, which has always been a subject of dispute among the Arab shaykhs because of its important water supply on an ancient trade route. As recently as 1955 Saudi Arabia occupied the Oasis, but was ejected when a British-led detachment of the Trucial Oman Scouts intervened on the side of Abu Dhabi. The Oasis was governed for twenty years by Shaykh Zayid of Abu Dhabi, before he became ruler of Abu Dhabi in 1966. Then Saudi interest in the Oasis led Abu Dhabi and Oman to reach an agreement on their borders and joint control of the Oasis.

The modern town of Abu Dhabi.

Each shaykh rules his own amirate and controls its mineral rights, taxes, and security force. However, the United Arab Amirates Constitution, promulgated in 1971, provides for a president and vice president of the federation to serve five-year terms, assisted by a prime minister and cabinet which has primary responsibility for drafting federal legislation. The Supreme Council of Rulers consists of the seven ruling shaykhs, in which each ruler has a vote, but both Abu Dhabi and Dubay have veto power. Meetings of the Supreme Council are held in Abu Dhabi, pending construction of a permanent capital astride the Abu Dhabi–Dubay border, and Shaykh Zayid of Abu Dhabi was selected as first president.

A National Council, made up of representatives appointed by the rulers for two-year terms, advises the federal government. No political parties exist, nor do any elected bodies or trade unions. However, each ruler must consider, to a certain degree, the relative strength of his family group and supporters in making decisions and appointments. The ruling families must, in turn, arrange stable alliances with other important families to secure their permanent support. In addition, Bedouin, although their numbers comprise only a small proportion of the population today, are important in the police and security forces in the shaykhdoms. Bedouin loyalty is still based on kinship ties, and their support is essential to maintaining the ruler's authority. Unfortunately, the more sophisticated town Arabs are inclined to look down on the rustic tribesmen, and the potential exists for clashes between the skilled immigrants in the labor force and the uneducated tribesmen who uphold the law. The rulers court tribal support by providing generous subsidies and housing for those who accept the time-honored obligation of acting as bodyguards and soldiers for the shaykh.

Rivalry between the ruling families is also a continuing problem. Before oil was discovered in Abu Dhabi in 1958, the tribes of the area were involved in constant bickering over control of trade, access to water holes, grazing rights, and fishing privileges as well as in internal conflicts over dynastic succession, leadership, and alliances among chiefs. Federation has by no means erased these long-standing sources of friction. At least twenty border areas within the United Arab Amirates have not yet been clearly demarcated. The ruler of Umm al Qaywayn claims that oil fields offshore belong to his shaykhdom rather than to Sharjah. A dozen and more conflicting claims over oil concession areas and sea boundaries between the shaykhdoms are still to be settled. Offshore boundaries with Iran are yet to be agreed upon.

However, the poor shaykhdoms are dependent on oil-rich Abu Dhabi for more than 90 percent of the United Arab Amirates' budget and realize that their economic and social development clearly depends on making the federation work.

The People's Democratic Republic of Yemen. One other area of former long-time British influence has not been covered—the Crown Colony of Aden and the adjacent Protectorates. Two developments in the 1950s led to British attempts to develop some sort of federation in Southern Yemen (as it became known to distinguish it from the Yemen Arab Republic). The closing of the Suez Canal in 1956 emphasized Britain's dependence on Persian Gulf oil and the need for a strong military base in Aden. But in 1958 the overthrow of the monarchy in Iraq in a bloody revolution suggested that the growing fervor of Arab nationalism would soon threaten the forces of empire.

In 1959 Britain set in motion the preparations for independence that included plans for a Federation of Southern Arabia, which would join the Crown Colony of Aden with the shaykhdoms in the two Protectorates. Not all of the tribal leaders liked the idea. The small poor shaykhdoms feared domination by the modern urban population of Aden, and Arab nationalists in Aden opposed continuing rule by traditional shaykhs who had relied on British protection to maintain their positions. The 1962 revolution in Yemen to the north further divided the factions for and against federation. Egyptian influence on the various nationalist leaders also alienated Adenis and tribal leaders alike.

Open terrorism broke out in 1965 between two nationalist groups, and the Arab-Israeli War in 1967 speeded Britain's decision to remove herself from the fray. She abandoned attempts to foster a federation, and began withdrawing forces from Aden and the Protectorates in 1967. Britain agreed to negotiate with any group capable of forming a government, and subsequently handed over control of Southern Yemen to an Arab nationalist movement called the National Liberation Front. The country became independent in 1967 and was named the People's Republic of Southern Yemen, but in 1969 the name was changed to the People's Democratic Republic of Yemen.

The name reflects the radical, left-wing orientation of the Front. The constitution of Southern Yemen, adopted in 1970, makes a 101-member appointed People's Supreme Council the country's legislature, but the National Liberation Front is the only political organization permitted. The People's Supreme Council enacts laws and elects the president, prime minister, and ministerial council. The president, prime minister, and chairman of the National Liberation Front comprise the Presidential Council, which is the actual center of power, aided by a ten-man executive committee of the official party.

The National Liberation Front is dedicated to the elimination of all Western economic influence from the Arabian Peninsula and the overthrow of the traditional rulers. However, the Front has been split by factional quarrels, and several at-

Women of the People's Democratic Republic of Yemen.

tempts to overthrow it led to the introduction of two or three thousand Cuban troops to train both guerilla fighters and a militia to protect the Front from army dissidents.

There is great economic, cultural, and educational disparity between the commercially oriented urban population of Aden (about two hundred fifty thousand people) and the tribes of the traditional agrarian interior, which has one of the lowest standards of living in the world. Political unrest has destroyed the once-important tourist trade, and the closing of the Suez Canal in 1967 dramatically reduced the thriving oil bunkering services which formerly made Aden one of the world's busiest ports. Now the economy is severely deflated, and this important commercial activity is unlikely to be revived to its former extent by the reopening of the Suez Canal in 1975 because much of the world's petroleum is now shipped in tankers too large to transit the Suez. The British Petroleum Company refinery at Aden still processes imported crude oil, but is operating at less than half capacity. It is, however, the single largest source of government income.

Although the People's Democratic Republic of Yemen avowed nonalignment as its attitude in international affairs, it cultivated close relations with radical nationalist Arab states, the USSR, and other Communist countries, and depended exclusively on the Soviet Union for military aid. Thus Southern Yemen became a breeding ground for trouble in the eyes of its more conservative neighbors, particularly after it permitted the Marxist-oriented Popular Front for the Liberation of Oman to operate out of Aden in conducting an insurgency in Dhofar Province of Oman. Relations with countries of the West were minimal after British military aid was terminated in 1968 and diplomatic relations with the United States severed in 1969.

However, in the spring of 1976 Saudi Arabia established diplomatic relations with Southern Yemen and indicated willingness to supply Southern Yemen with military and economic aid. Interdependence within the Peninsula will, it is hoped, replace Southern Yemen's dependence on Communist countries for support.

8

Politics

The governments of all the independent states in the Arabian Peninsula are elitist in the sense that each state is ruled by a small group of leaders and the general population is not involved in shaping political ideologies. Bahrayn and Kuwayt have moved the furthest toward constitutional government by instituting elected national assemblies, but since no political parties are permitted, the members are apt to be chosen from the upper strata of society. The United Arab Amirates have a consultative assembly to advise the shaykhs, but it is appointed by the shaykhs. Saudi Arabia, Qatar, and Oman are traditional tribal monarchies. The two Yemens are governed by presidential councils, and they are the furthest to the left in political philosophy of any of the Peninsula governments. Governments in both believe Yemen should be reunited, but neither wants to surrender its power.

Aside from the Yemens, all the nations of the Peninsula have traditional rulers, drawn from leading families which have enjoyed high tribal rank for decades. Foreigners who do not understand the tribal system often criticize this kind of rule for being authoritarian. However, the highly personalized rule of the Arab chieftains has always been and still is widely accepted by the people who are ruled by them. Moslem law is accepted by Moslems as a just system of law.

Peninsula Arabs feel that they have access to their rulers and that their wants and needs are heeded and their rights protected. Any citizen can come to the ruler's daily *majlis*, stand before or sit down beside him, call him by his first name, and petition him for help or ask assistance in righting a wrong. The ruler's personal attention to each citizen's individual problems becomes increasingly difficult in a country as big as Saudi Arabia, but even there the Saudis have direct access to the king or to his close associates, a situation which does not exist in most constitutional republics. The Saudis cherish this kind of benevolent rule and feel involved in it.

The Arab rulers are by no means all-powerful autocrats. They are not even hereditary monarchs; succession may be within one particular family, but it does not pass automatically from father to son. The most capable or astute male member of the family is put on the throne, and he rules by consent and the force of his personality. He is regarded as first among equals, and will be removed if his leadership falls short of the expectations of his peers. A fair number of leaders are involved in the decision as to who shall succeed to the chiefship, including not only the powerful members of the ruling family but also the traditional scholars of Moslem law who are the *qadis* of Islamic courts, members of leading mercantile families, tribal chiefs and shaykhs of other important families and Bedouin clans. To this group is being added a growing number of local bureaucrats and university graduates whose intellectual skills permit them to move rapidly into the top strata of society.

Admittedly the route to power is determined by birth or by possession of select skills, which limits the circle that partici-

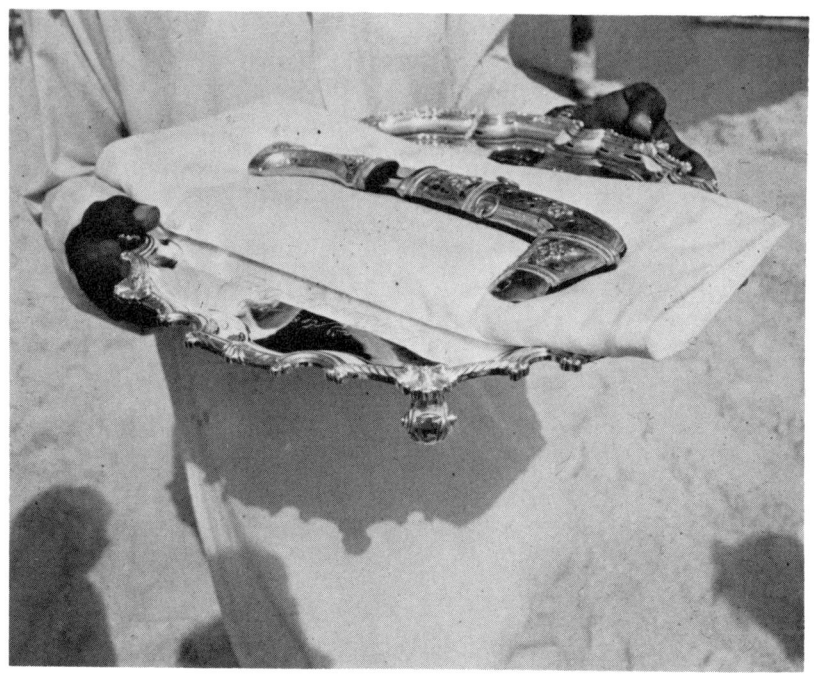

Ceremonial dagger worn by the ruler of Dubay at the launching of an underwater oil storage tank.

pates in political activity and hinders the development of wide popular interest in the exercise of power. Traditional rule is possible when there are no political parties, no elections, no trade unions, no interest groups, no free press, and when government controls information media so that any revolutionary ideas are strictly limited. These are all restrictions that hinder the growth of political awareness.

Traditional rule has succeeded in maintaining stability in the Peninsula largely because expectations have not risen faster than the rulers' ability to meet them, thanks to oil wealth. In fact, this is the only region in the world where great natural resource wealth and small populations make it possible for government to provide everything people could desire in the way of social services without their having to demand them. In other developing countries, even those possessing substantial natural resource wealth, populations are so much greater that choices always have to be made as to where to allocate resources to build transportation networks, schools, hospitals, and the rest, because there simply is not enough money or skills to provide all these things for everyone. Those who get them are pleased. Those who don't become dissatisfied and frustrated; either they turn to political agitation in search of their fair share, or incipient opposition is repressed by police and military forces. Social services generally go first to urban areas where larger populations can be served, with the result that impoverished rural workers flock to the cities seeking jobs and living standards that simply don't exist.

Not all of the Peninsula countries are equally endowed, of course, but sharing is an honored Arab tradition. Saudi Arabia, Kuwayt, Qatar, Abu Dhabi, and Dubay have consistently aided their neighbors. Bahrayn and Oman can absorb all their own oil revenues and more, while the non-oil shaykhdoms of the United Arab Amirates and the two Yemens need very substantial help. Fortunately, oil is bringing in sufficient income to meet all their needs, and there would be much logic in forming some sort of Peninsula-wide economic federation to plan the wisest use and distribution of resources. This has not yet been considered, and probably will not happen as long as dynastic rivalries, territorial disputes, and differences in political ideology cause strains among the countries of the Peninsula.

RELATIONS WITHIN THE ARABIAN PENINSULA

Because of Saudi Arabia's size and her substantial oil wealth, her relations with her smaller neighbors are of considerable importance to them. The fact that few of the interior borders around the Empty Quarter of Saudi Arabia have been defined is an automatic source of tension. Saudi Arabia's ties to other Peninsula states are closest where there are no border disputes to muddy the waters, and when strong religious and kin ties are shared.

Bahrayn is an excellent example. Offshore boundaries have been defined, permitting Saudi Arabia and Bahrayn to share revenues from the Abu Safa oil field, and crude oil from the Saudi mainland is refined in the Bahrayn Petroleum Company refinery on Bahrayn. Bahrayn has extensive trade with Saudi Arabia. These close economic ties are doubtless facilitated by the fact that the ruling families of the two countries, the Al Saud and the Al Khalifa, trace their origins to the same clan of the famous Anayzah tribal confederation of north central Arabia. The ruler of Bahrayn has long looked to the king of Saudi Arabia for both leadership and political support.

Relations between Saudi Arabia and Kuwayt are also close. Borders were defined many years ago, and more recently an agreement was made to divide the Neutral Zone between them and share the oil resources there. The ruling families respect each other and have no quarrels. Saudi Arabia and Qatar also have related ruling families and share a well-established border. They share strong religious ties, both following the same Moslem school of law. Qatar follows Saudi lead in international affairs, and trusts Saudis well enough to employ them in her security forces. Relations may not be as intimate as between Saudi Arabia and Bahrayn, but they are serene.

Saudi Arabia's relations with the United Arab Amirates have been marred by the long-standing dispute over the Al Buraymi Oasis; some of the indigenous tribes supported Saudi Arabia's claim to the oasis because of Wahhabi religious ties. King Faysal refused to recognize the United Arab Amirates upon independence, and it was only after the Buraymi quarrel was settled in 1974 that diplomatic relations were finally established and efforts made to develop joint policies on oil and regional security. Both sides now seem to recognize that stability and internal calm are in their best interests. Saudi Arabia is concerned over the welfare of the large number of Wahhabi Moslems living in the United Arab Amirates, but prefers now to work with the union government rather than act disruptively.

Saudi Arabia and Yemen have a long history of friction over their undefined interior borders, because what happens in the mountains of Yemen has substantial impact on the people of Asir Province of Saudi Arabia. For religious and ideological reasons the Saudis supported the imam of Yemen in the civil war against the republicans and their Egyptian supporters, and that involvement was ended only after repeated negotiations between Saudi Arabia and Egypt and the 1967 Arab-Israeli War, which distracted Egypt's attention to her own major problems. The civil war in Yemen has pretty much petered out, and Saudi Arabia has been providing financial assistance to the republican government to build schools, hospitals, water facilities, and roads, which will benefit both countries economically.

Relations between Saudi Arabia and Southern Yemen were practically non-existent until 1976, because the Saudis mistrusted the radical socialist ideology of the National Liberation Front and its active espousal of a movement to rid the Peninsula of all traditional autocratic governments. However, diplomatic relations have now been established and Saudi economic aid promised to Southern Yemen.

Saudi Arabia and Oman share a fair number of Bedouin tribesmen who roam freely in the interior between the Hajar Mountains and the Empty Quarter, but these tribesmen are such an independent bunch that their activities are not really controlled by either government. The Saudis are concerned about the revolutionary guerilla action that has been going on in Dhofar Province of Oman, but the Sultan of Oman turned to Iran and Jordan for military help rather than to Saudi Arabia. However, he is dependent on his oil-rich neighbors for economic help, since Oman's oil resources are very limited.

Kuwayt is a giant in oil wealth, but a midget in area and population. Her relations with her neighbors are predominantly economic and cultural, and Kuwayt has been very generous in sharing her oil revenues. Ties with Bahrayn are very close because of long tribal and trade connections. There are economic and technical cooperation agreements between the two and a joint investment bank. Bahrayn looks to both Kuwayt and Saudi Arabia for financial and military assistance.

Kuwayt has no disputes with the United Arab Amirates, and has extended considerable financial aid since 1954, thus making a very positive impact and somewhat muting dynastic rivalries. Her less fortunate neighbors send students to Kuwayt University and look to Kuwayt for educational, cultural, and commercial leadership.

The shaykhs of the United Arab Amirates resent claims by

Kuwayt City.

other ruling families of the Peninsula to more aristocratic lineages than theirs. Such resentment is lessened when neighbors like Saudi Arabia and Kuwayt provide generous assistance. The Qatar rulers particularly resent memories of the days when the Bahrayn shaykhs occupied Qatar, and these deep dynastic rivalries prevented the larger federation that Britain hoped in the 1960s to achieve among the nine protected Gulf shaykhdoms. Both Bahrayn and Qatar also claim the Hawar Islands, and this kind of territorial dispute always strains relations.

Qatar and the United Arab Amirates have settled boundary disputes between them, but their leaders are still competing to provide leadership for the Lower Gulf. Relations between Qatar and Dubay in particular are strained because Dubay granted asylum to Shaykh Ahmad of Qatar, whom Shaykh Khalifa deposed in 1972.

In the southern region of the Peninsula the revolt in Dhofar has made both the Southern Yemenis and the Omanis suspect in Saudi Arabia and the Gulf shaykhdoms where no radicals are wanted. The Soviet Union has been the main supplier of arms to Southern Yemen and the Dhofar rebels, a fact that is resented by other Peninsula Arabs. Fortunately the intervention of Iran has allowed Oman to take much of the steam out of the rebellion so that it is no longer a major security menace in the region. The Dhofar insurgency has also spurred the other governments to the north to strive for rapid political and socioeconomic improvements in their own countries as the best way of discouraging revolutionary trends.

ARAB UNITY

The spread of the Moslem religion was responsible for the original diffusion of Arab culture, but the idea of an Arab identity is a fairly recent development. The first stirrings of Arab nationalism occurred in Syria in the nineteenth century and were very much a revolt against domination by the Ottoman Turks. This was the same period in which the concept of the nation-state was coming to the fore in Europe, and the idea was disseminated by European education, carried to the Moslem world by Christian missionaries.

The Wahhabi movement in Arabia was also an attempt to drive out the Ottoman Turks. Arab literature of the nineteenth century began to reflect such reform movements as it sought to revive classical Arabic language and history and to express the conflict between traditionalists (like the Wahhabis) and modernists, who hoped to add vitality to Arab culture by adopting some of the ideas of the West.

The idea that there is a single Arab heritage and that all Arabs should be united is an intellectual concept that was borrowed from the West around the turn of the twentieth century by the educated Arab elite. It is practically meaningless to the illiterate peasant who identifies himself according to his religious sect, his family, and the region in which he lives. Leaders in the Arab world have made any number of attempts to put together unions of Arab countries, only to have them founder because of power struggles among the leaders.

World War II spurred Arab leaders to try to cooperate in supporting their demands for independence, and led to the formation of the Arab League by Egypt, Syria, Lebanon, Iraq, Transjordan, and Saudi Arabia in 1945. But the League was no more able to arbitrate dynastic rivalries than the colonial powers had been, and unity was achieved only on those issues where the members' interests coincided. The containment of Israel was one of the few questions on which the Arabs could agree. Internal politics divided the Arab governments when the growth of revolutionary socialism in Egypt, Syria, and Iraq alarmed the traditional hereditary monarchs. Egypt's solicitation of Russian help and arms under President Nasser contrasted sharply with Saudi Arabia's friendship with the United States. Such policies were new variations on the old struggles by contending parties for leadership of the Arab world. Yet Egypt cooperated with Saudi Arabia to keep Iraq from taking

An Arab from the State of Qatar.

over Kuwayt in 1961, and it was no coincidence that the Kuwayt Fund for Arab Economic Development began in 1962 to make large grants to the countries like Egypt which had supported it.

However, it was not until the 1967 Arab-Israeli War that the split between the "revolutionary" pan-Arabists and the traditional rulers was papered over by Egyptian agreement to withdraw from Yemen. The death of Nasser in 1970 permitted the succession of a moderate Egyptian leader, General Anwar Sadat, and in the 1973 war with Israel the Arabs for the first time demonstrated real military capability. The success of OPEC in raising oil prices and the effectiveness of the Arab oil embargo against the developed nations have given a big boost to Arab unity. In 1976 Saudi Arabia, Kuwayt, and the United Arab Amirates agreed to help Egypt repay her debts to the Soviet Union, which the Russians refused to reschedule.

ISRAEL

The quarrel between the Arabs and the Israelis cannot be adequately covered in a few paragraphs. The barest outline is that the Zionist movement, which sought a homeland for the world's Jews, gained a promise from Britain in 1917 (the Balfour Declaration) that they could have a homeland in Palestine, over which Britain acquired a League of Nations mandate after World War I. At the same time Britain promised that the rights of non-Jewish communities would be protected. Jewish immigration to Palestine grew steadily thereafter, although Arabs within Palestine increasingly opposed a growing number of foreigners settling in their midst. However, the Nazi persecution of Jews in Europe provided an urgent impetus for the creation of a Jewish refuge that took precedence over self-determination for the indigenous Palestinians.

In 1947 the United Nations General Assembly, by a very close margin, voted to end the British mandate and temporarily partition Palestine between Arabs and Jews. On May 15, 1948, the Jewish National Council announced the existence of the State of Israel, and its independence was recognized by the Great Powers. At the same time the surrounding Arab states declared war, and in the ensuing conflict seven hundred thousand Arabs whose homes and land were within the newly formed Israel chose to flee, either from fear or unwillingness to remain as second-class citizens under a government which was not of their choosing. Population moved in both directions; Arabs left Israel, while Jews moved from Arab lands into Israel. The Arab refugees were settled in camps in Lebanon, Syria, Jordan, and the Gaza Strip, and have been cared for ever since by a United Nations Works and Relief Agency financed by voluntary contributions.

In the 1947 war only the Arab Legion of Transjordan put up a real fight, seizing the left bank of the Jordan River and part of Jerusalem. Eventually the Arabs were soundly defeated. In a series of ensuing conflicts the Israelis have seized all of Jerusalem and the left bank of the Jordan from the state of Jordan, the Golan Heights from Syria, the Gaza Strip from a United Nations force, and the Sinai Peninsula from Egypt. However, the Arabs demonstrated a greatly improved military capability in the fourth Arab-Israeli War in 1973, which has resulted in a new spirit of Arab cooperation.

The costliness of repeated conflict has led moderate Arab leaders in Egypt, Jordan, and the Arabian Peninsula to modify their earlier demands for Israel's eradication. They have indicated willingness to accept a permanent settlement with Israel if the agreement is based on UN Resolution 242, which requires Israel's return to the 1967 borders. The Arabs also want a separate state for the Palestinian Arabs, and internationalization of Jerusalem, which is regarded as holy by Moslems as well as Christians.

The problem of a homeland for the stateless Palestinians has become more urgent as their numbers have grown to over 3 million. Of this number 450,000 live in Israel as second-class citizens; 1,500,000 live in UNWRA refugee camps; and 1,050,000 in lands seized by the Israelis in the 1967 war. Many others are working in Arab countries.

The situation has been complicated by Great Power arming of the combatants. The United States supplies arms to Israel, Jordan, and Saudi Arabia, while Russia aided Egypt in the 1960s and still provides arms to Syria and Iraq. Today oil wealth enables Arab nations like Saudi Arabia and Kuwayt to pay cash for immense quantities of weapons and transfer them to whomever they please.

Oil in this situation becomes a double-edged weapon. It not only provides the wherewithal to arm and fight, but also forces the industrial nations, which need oil so badly, to try to defuse tensions in the Middle East so that oil will continue to flow. Effective use of this weapon is complicated and requires great skill and international statesmanship on the part of the Arabs who are wielding it.

Long-term stability in the Arabian Peninsula will require, of course, a settlement of the Arab quarrel with Israel which permits both the Arabs and Israelis to feel secure. This will necessitate compromise and adjustment by all parties involved, which includes not only Israel and her immediate neighbors with whom she has border quarrels, but all the Arab states. All Arab leaders today embrace strong sentiments of Arab nationalism, which have been given cohesion by the Zionist presence on territory which had belonged to Arab Moslems for centuries. The ties of Arab blood and Moslem faith line up the countries of the Arabian Peninsula solidly behind the Palestinian Arabs. The presence of well-educated and articulate Palestinians working in all the cities of the Peninsula is a constant reminder of these ties. The Arab oil countries have contributed substantially over the years to the relief of Palestinian refugees, and more recently to the arming of the Palestinian Liberation Organization.

RELATIONS WITH NEIGHBORS

Iraq. There is little sympathy in the Arabian Peninsula for Iraq's brand of radical socialism or for her ties with the Soviet Union. In 1972 Iraq and the USSR signed a fifteen-year treaty of friendship, and Russia is the main supplier of arms to Iraq. Because Soviet ships berth in Iraq, Bahrayn permits a small United States Navy presence in her harbor.

Iraq has never formally relinquished its claim to Kuwayt, although the claim has not been pressed recently. Iraq and Iran have settled their major differences over the confluence of the Tigris and Euphrates Rivers, bringing an atmosphere of greater serenity to the Upper Gulf. At the same time Iraq, Syria, and Egypt have been too preoccupied with domestic issues and with the aftermath of the 1973 war with Israel to involve themselves in Peninsula affairs, except to court the wealthy oil rulers for financial assistance. The sharing of oil wealth among the Arab states has added considerable strength to the long-sought-for goal of Arab unity. Qatar, for example, has provided both economic and military assistance to Egypt, while in return Egypt has contributed substantial technical services to Qatar's education system. This kind of bilateral assistance between nations of the region cannot help but diminish frictions.

Nevertheless, the principal threats to traditional rulers from radical ideologies seem to come from Iraq and Southern Yemen, both allied with Russia. Saudi Arabia and Iran are the two strong states confronting that threat in the Gulf, both of them supplied mainly by United States arms. The King of Saudi Arabia and the Shah of Iran settled their differences in 1968 when Britain began withdrawing from the Gulf, and both want to promote stability there—not an impossible objective if neither the Arabs or the Iranians get embroiled in a controversy which is contrary to the interests of the other.

Iran. Iran has indicated its intention of guaranteeing the security of the Gulf in order to protect its oil resources and the free flow of shipping, which makes its position more important to the Arabian Peninsula than that of other neighboring states. Unfortunately, there are suspicions of very long standing between the Iranians (Persians) and the Arabs in the Gulf, resulting particularly from disagreements over territorial limits and their application to the many islands of the Gulf. The Gulf is not wide enough to divide equitably, and the continental shelf is continuous from one coast to the other. Even if a median line could be drawn, the many offshore islands confuse any such demarcation. In addition, the discovery of offshore oil fields and new methods of exploiting them makes seabed rights a matter of vital economic importance.

Negotiations with Iran have produced compromises for Iraq, Kuwayt, and Saudi Arabia, and have considerably muted Arab fears of Iranian domination. Iran has also recently relinquished a two-centuries-old claim to Bahrayn, which has narrowed the differences between those two states. But parts of the median line in the Gulf between Iran and other Arab states have not yet been agreed upon, and when the United Arab Amirates became independent in 1971 conflicting claims

Aerial view of tidal fish traps in the Gulf along the eastern coast of Saudi Arabia.

were heightened as Iran occupied Abu Musa and the two Tunbs Islands, which the Arabs regard as belonging to the amirates. The ruler of Sharjah was later assassinated for signing an agreement with the Shah of Iran permitting occupation of Abu Musa.

Other factors besides territory enter into Arab relations with Iran. There is the centuries-old cleavage between the Sunni branch of Islam, to which the Arabs generally adhere, and the Shia branch, which predominates in Iran. On the other hand, there are strong commercial ties, with Iranian merchants and laborers particularly numerous in the Gulf shaykhdoms.

Iran's friendly relationship to Israel clashes head-on with Arab nationalism, particularly because Iran supplied oil to Israel during the 1973 war and the Arab oil embargo, and because the Iranian Navy at that time protected Western tankers going to and from her refinery at Abadan. Growing economic and commercial ties between Iran and the Arab states in the Gulf since then have pretty much counterbalanced this, but another Arab-Israeli war could seriously disrupt Arab relations with Iran.

Barring such a conflict, Iran, Iraq, and the Arab states all have a vital stake in the free passage of ships through the Gulf and the Strait of Hormuz, for this is the lifeline for export of their oil. This is why the Shah of Iran stepped in to help the Sultan of Oman put down the rebellion in Dhofar Province; none of the Gulf states can tolerate the possibility of an unfriendly government in Oman cutting off shipping through the Strait.

Pakistan. Relations between the states of the Arabian Peninsula and Pakistan are particularly close because they share the emotional solidarity of being Sunni Moslems. There are no historical animosities or territorial disputes to mar the harmony. Large numbers of Pakistanis are employed in both skilled and unskilled jobs throughout the Gulf countries. Pathans and Baluchis from Pakistan are trusted members of the security forces of the Lower Gulf, and Pakistan has military training missions in Saudi Arabia and Abu Dhabi.

Africa. The Arab and African states have combined forces on international political issues about which they feel very strongly. The Arabs supported Africans in getting South Africa barred from the United Nations General Assembly in 1974 because of its apartheid policy, and Africans supported the Arabs in achieving the attendance of the Palestine Liberation Organization at the United Nations and the condemnation of Zionism by the General Assembly as a form of racism.

An Arab loan fund has provided small amounts of money to Uganda, Tanzania, Liberia, and Zambia, and an Arab Development Bank for Africa has been formed. The Africans are unhappy that Arab oil producers have not yet granted special treatment in the way of lowered oil prices to Africans, as Nigeria has. Although OPEC has set up a $1 billion loan fund to help poor oil-consuming states, the Arabs have not yet developed continuing economic aid programs. Direct loans from oil countries, such as those made to Mauretania by Saudi Arabia and Kuwayt, have had more political impact.

Africans and Arabians alike are concerned with the approach to the Red Sea between Africa and the Arabian Peninsula. The Bab al-Mandeb Strait is a narrow maritime passage divided into two channels by Perim Island. International traffic passes into and out of the Red Sea through the western channel, two miles off Perim and seven miles from the African coast. Ships must traverse the territorial waters of four states to make the passage: The Yemen Arab Republic and the People's Democratic Republic of Yemen on the east; on the west Ethiopia and the French Territory of Afars and Issas.

Since the Suez Canal reopened in 1975, this strait is of great strategic importance. The People's Democratic Republic of Yemen has sovereignty over Perim Island. The question of free passage through the strait was discussed at the 1974 Law of the Sea Conference, and international control of the strait suggested, but pressure against any international arrangement is coming increasingly from the two Yemens, Ethiopia, Oman, the Arab League, the Organization of African Unity, the Afro-Asian Consultative Organization, and the like, because any outside settlement might endanger national security interests.

EXTERNAL RELATIONS

Britain. British influence varies in her former protectorates in the Arabian Peninsula. British commercial interests in the oil refinery in Aden are about the only residue of the colonial era in Southern Yemen. In the Gulf shaykhdoms, in contrast, British influence is still substantial, not only in the form of commercial and petroleum activities, but also because British advisers and contract personnel still work within the independent governments and British officers lead security forces in Bahrayn, Qatar, the United Arab Amirates, and Oman.

United States. Because of major involvement in the oil industry, the United States has played a leading role in the Arabian Peninsula since World War II. The United States has also had a military aid mission in Saudi Arabia since 1951, and in 1956 agreed to train, equip, and help double in size the Saudi army

Muttrah, a seaport on the coast of Oman.

and navy. The United States has also become the major supplier of arms to the whole Gulf region, which involves American technicians and training personnel in large numbers, and the facilities to support them. These multi-billion-dollar arms sales have benefited the American international balance of payments position, partly offsetting costly, increasing purchases of Arab oil. However, questions should be asked as to whether arms purchases are a good use of Arab resources.

Relations between the United States and the Arab states are very much complicated by American policies which have generally supported Israel. By 1976 the United States had provided Israel with about a billion dollars in economic aid, mostly before 1965, and $3.5 billion in military aid, mostly since 1972, with similar amounts promised in the future as part of the Sinai agreement. Granting military aid to one side while selling massive amounts of armaments to the other, which can afford to pay cash for such purchases because of oil wealth, makes further conflict a constant threat.

Both sides claim that their weapons needs are purely defensive, but the 1973 Arab-Israeli War, the resulting five-month oil embargo, and vast Arab oil wealth have made it clear that Middle East problems are no longer bilateral, and we must sort out our attitudes toward the unresolved conflict in the Middle East. These realities have demonstrated how dangerous it is for us to be insensitive to the needs and fears of the peoples of the Arabian Peninsula.

Soviet Union. Southern Yemen is the only country on the Arabian Peninsula where revolutionary socialism has gained a foothold with Soviet aid and arms. Southern Yemen's neighbors fear disruptive threats to their stability through internal subversion both from that direction and from the north where Iraq and Syria are also armed by the USSR. The traditional Arab monarchies dislike Communism because of its antireligious bias, and do not permit Communist organizations to function. Only Kuwayt has diplomatic relations with Communist countries. Saudi Arabia states forthrightly that her foreign policy is to cooperate with all peace-loving nations which believe in God. Islam and Communism are incompatible ideologies, and Arab governments will remain anti-

Communist as long as their rulers stoutly maintain the predominance of Moslem law. The threat comes from movements dedicated to the overthrow of the Moslem idealists.

Soviet interest in the Middle East is not based on energy needs, for Russia is the only major power producing more oil at home than it needs. Russia would consider another disruption in the flow of Arab oil to the industrial nations a victory for revolutionary socialism. The situation may change in a decade or so, but at the present time the Soviet Union seeks to encourage revolutionary movements wherever possible. The USSR supports the Arabs in their quarrel with Israel and offers Soviet weapons to nations such as Kuwayt, which fear that United States policies in the Middle East might leave them stranded.

Japan and Europe. Japan and the industrialized countries of Western Europe are eager to participate in the economic boom in the oil-producing countries. Businessmen from all over the world, generally with strong home government support, are in almost every Peninsula country contracting, or seeking contracts, for the sale of their goods and services.

9

Oil

Within the last fifty years the discovery and exploitation of a natural resource, petroleum, has affected the way of life of the people of the Arabian Peninsula almost beyond belief. How has the development of a single industry become the most important factor affecting political, economic, and social affairs of an entire region—indeed, of the whole world, perhaps?

The utilization of petroleum as the lubrication and energy source of industrial society has occurred only in the last century, although its existence is nothing new. The Old Testament refers a number of times to oil and gas seepages such as the fiery furnace of Shadrach, Meshach, and Abednego. Noah caulked his ark with pitch or bitumen. Archeologists in their excavations have confirmed that ancient peoples used petroleum as mortar, for waterproofing, as medicine, and as fuel for lamps.

The development of mechanized factories in Europe and the United States in the nineteenth century created a growing demand for lubricants and lighting oils. Sources of petroleum in the United States had been known before, but not until 1859 was a well dug in Pennsylvania for the specific purpose of mining oil. A successful strike there launched an industry that has revolutionized man's way of life.

Within a decade oil was being produced in Russia, Rumania, Canada, and Italy, and by 1900, Burma, Poland, Japan, Germany, India, Peru, and Indonesia had been added to the list, followed shortly by Mexico, Argentina, Trinidad, and Iran. In those early years the principal petroleum products were kerosene for lamps and stoves, and lubricants for machinery. Not until the development of the internal combustion engine led to the growth of the automotive industry did a rapidly expanding demand for gasoline and other petroleum products turn the petroleum industry into a highly sophisticated operation. In the 1920s the navies of the world were converted to oil, followed by the world's merchant fleets.

A tremendous expansion of the petroleum industry was fired by a world-wide switch from coal to cheap fossil fuels as a source of energy after World War II. The industry of Europe was rebuilt, switching from coal to oil for fuel. Automobiles became the common mode of transportation in the United States and Europe. Other areas of the world turned to petroleum as their energy source as they adopted Western patterns of earning a living and of transportation. Japan, for example, rebuilt her society on the United States model after the war and became a major consumer. Rising expectations in the Middle East, Latin America, Asia, and Africa led to a steadily increasing demand for oil for industry, roads, motor vehicles, mechanized agriculture, fertilizers, electric generators, plastics, kerosene for heating, and the multiple other modern conveniences that are made possible by petroleum.

The petroleum industry is highly competitive, nowhere better illustrated than in the jockeying by the major oil companies to obtain from Middle Eastern governments agreements called concessions, which permitted them to explore for oil in certain areas. The Turkish Petroleum Company was formed before World War I by companies of several European nations to prospect for oil in what is now Iraq. After the discovery of oil there, it became the Iraq Petroleum Company.

Several American oil companies were searching for oil abroad in the 1920s. Standard Oil of California (SOCAL) chartered the Bahrayn Petroleum Company, Ltd., in Canada in 1930, and discovered oil in Bahrayn two years later. Having established a good reputation, SOCAL then negotiated an agreement with King Abdul Aziz ibn Saud of Saudi Arabia to explore the east coast region, just twenty miles away from Bahrayn Island. SOCAL formed the California Arabian Standard Oil Company to exploit the concession, and the name was changed in 1944 to the Arabian American Oil Company (Aramco). In 1936 the Texas Company combined its marketing facilities with SOCAL's production facilities to become half owner of Aramco.

In 1934 the Anglo-Iranian/Gulf Oil group discovered an enormous oil field to the north in Kuwayt. The era of oil in the Peninsula had begun.

Oil exploration is an enormously expensive and complicated undertaking, especially when it is attempted in a harsh and barren desert, miles from any facilities whatsoever. The oil fields in the Arabian Peninsula are generally located in regions where only nomadic herdsmen can survive by moving their flocks from one patch of scrub grass to another. There were no permanent settlements except for a few fishing villages, tiny harbors, and small administrative towns whose growth had been encouraged by the handful of activities connected with Britain's protectorate system in the Gulf shaykhdoms.

Although each oil company faced and coped with a particular set of problems connected with the country or shaykhdom in which it operated, the experience of Aramco in developing one of the world's largest oil fields is perhaps typical. The first geologists came by boat from Bahrayn, went ashore in eastern Arabia, and used camels to transport their equipment to their first camp in the coastal village called Dammam. A total of eight men attempted to pinpoint the best spots to drill for oil in a concession that covered 320,000 square miles. An airplane finally arrived from the States with two more men to do aerial observations and photographs needed for more detailed geological studies. Other wildcatters with different skills straggled in, recruited from jobs all over the world. After two years' surface examination of the terrain, this small handful of prospectors decided that the Dammam Dome was a structure similar to the one already yielding oil on Bahrayn Island. That was the spot to test.

Next came engineers, construction men, and drillers. They had to be housed and supplied with both equipment and food, none of which was available in eastern Arabia. Every last item they needed had to be shipped 11,000 miles from the United States and be in place when they needed it. The small fishing village of Al Khobar was selected as the site for a rock pier, built by Saudi work crews from the shore through the shoals into deeper water where small boats and barges could unload. A rough road was built to connect the port and the drilling site, while a camp was being constructed at Dhahran to house the workmen. Between 1934 and 1937 Aramco drilled seven

An oil exploration camp in Abu Dhabi.

test holes without finding oil in commercial quantities. The seventh hole was started in 1936, and again yielded no oil. Only when the hunch of one of the wildcatters led them to go deeper—to almost five thousand feet—did liquid gold finally gush out of the sand.

Finding the oil was only the first step in the process. A community had to be built to house the much larger work staff which would be involved in the production of oil. In Dhahran dormitories, cottages, and apartments were erected for the crews and their families. Since the town was sitting out in the open desert with nothing but sand in every direction, the community required a dining hall, a clubhouse, and a swimming pool for recreation, a commissary for shopping, storehouses for supplies, repair shops to maintain heavy equipment, garages for the vehicles, a laundry, a utility plant to supply electricity, a central air-conditioning plant to make life bearable in the desert heat. A storage and shipping terminal had to be constructed to ship the oil, and a pipeline to get it from the well to the port. The first oil was sent by barge to the Bahrayn Petroleum Company refinery twenty-five miles away.

If oil was to be shipped elsewhere, a facility to load tankers was needed. Ras Tanura was chosen for a marine terminal. A larger pipeline, storage tanks, pumps, moorings, and submarine loading lines were constructed to an anchorage over half a mile offshore where water was deep enough to receive ocean-going vessels. A large stabilizer plant was completed in Dhahran to remove poisonous hydrogen sulfide gas before the crude oil could be shipped.

Shipping difficulties, tanker shortages, and inaccessibility of markets during World War II brought Aramco operations almost to a halt. Wives and children were sent home, and a skeleton staff remained behind to supply crude oil to the Bahrayn refinery. The employees who remained found other activities to keep them busy. They did a survey of water resources in the Al Kharj area southeast of Riyadh, which made possible the reclamation and irrigation of an extensive tract for agriculture. They kept their scant fleet of vehicles running with ingenuity and whatever parts they could rig up, and used them for emergency food hauling service when a severe drought threatened the Arabs. They fattened their own sheep and cattle for food, turned one of their air-conditioned cottages into a brooder for hatching chickens, and grew their own vegetables.

By 1943 the American war effort was requiring enormous quantities of oil, and the United States government allocated materials to construct a refinery at Ras Tanura, plus the needed trucks and construction equipment. The project included storage tanks, loading lines, a T-shaped pier with large tanker berths, and a submarine pipeline to the Bahrayn refinery, which was being enlarged. The quiet of Aramco's holding operation in Dhahran turned almost overnight into pandemonium, as men struggled to cope with both the complications of a large construction project far from its supplies and the confusion of getting scarce items in wartime.

The refinery went into operation in 1945, and by the end of that year Aramco had discovered two more oil fields—Abu Hadriya and Qatif. With the end of the war, production was rapidly increased. In 1951 Aramco discovered its first offshore reservoir 150 miles north of Dhahran; called Safaniya, it is one of the largest in the world. Important new discoveries followed in the late 1950s. In 1951 the Saudi government paid Aramco to build a railroad from Dammam to Riyadh. By

1974 there were 300 wells operating in sixteen different fields, with all the required equipment, support services, crews, pipelines, and the rest.

All this expansion in production necessitated expansion in facilities—enlarged marine terminals, including a tanker-loading sea island; more storage tanks; more stabilization plants; a greatly expanded electric power grid. Enlarged and more efficient refinery capacity was provided at Ras Tanura, which processes crude oil, a mixture of hydrocarbons ranging from the lightest gases to the heaviest asphalts, by separating it into useful components which can be blended and treated to make consumer products—naphtha and light gases (mostly propane and butane), kerosene, light and heavy diesel oils, fuel oils, jet fuel, and asphalt. These products are further separated by distillation, and various combinations of their components reformed to make gasoline. New processes were begun, such as the production and export of natural gas liquids (propane, butane, and natural gas), and gas injection plants were built to return compressed gas into oil-bearing formations so that natural energy forces oil to the surface without pumping.

Exploration parties in the Empty Quarter began using helicopters, air-conditioned trailers, sand buggies with oversize low-pressure tires, and truck convoys to regularly supply exploration camps in the trackless desert. In addition to hunting for oil, the geologists produced maps of all of Saudi Arabia in collaboration with the Saudi and United States governments. The application of advanced engineering and scientific principles to oil production led to the extensive use of computers to study reservoir conditions requiring gas and liquid injection programs, to work out decisions as to where and when to drill wells, and the like.

Even the production of petroleum and its refining for ship-

Aerial view of Ahmadi, a modern town created by the oil industry in Kuwayt.

ment was not the end of the spectrum of activities undertaken by Aramco. To make oil available in Europe at minimum prices, Aramco's owner companies decided to build a 754-mile pipeline from the oil fields to Sidon on the Mediterranean coast in Lebanon. The construction of the Trans-Arabian Pipeline (Tapline) involved the same complex logistics in moving men and supplies into place across a rugged, largely deserted terrain, where roads, camps, water, food, and transport all had to be arranged from scratch. Finished in 1950, Tapline has complete communities to man the five pump stations, with repair shops, supply depots, airstrips, communications, housing, hospitals, schools, feeding and recreation facilities, utilities, offices, and roads. These facilities have attracted Arab settlers to the point that these pump stations are now centers of flourishing towns.

Facilities are only half the picture, however. Producing, refining, and shipping oil, plus all the support services involved, requires a wide range of human resources, and it would be neither economical nor good for the host country to have all the manpower required brought in from overseas. In a region like eastern Arabia, inhabited by nomadic herdsmen, the only way to utilize local manpower was to train it and to provide the social services requisite to employment in the sedentary oil industry. In the beginning training was informal, on-the-job teaching of drillers, craftsmen, office workers. To this kind of apprenticeship training was soon added academic and craftshop classroom programs. Later the company began paying for employee education or advanced vocational training overseas. Industrial Training Centers were established at Abqaiq, Dhahran, Ras Tanura, Dammam, and Al Hasa, to give instruction both on company time and in the evenings in Arabic and English, math, the sciences, social studies, and operation of business machines. By 1975 more than fifty-five hundred Saudi Arab employees were enrolled in training programs.

In the beginning Aramco built not only offices and shops, but also roads, utilities, clinics, recreation facilities, houses, and schools. It acted as grocer, banker, laundryman, shoemaker, maintenance mechanic, and all the rest. The company soon embarked on employee training programs, began giving technical and financial assistance to businesses and industrial concerns, helped in the development of agriculture and medical care, offered employees home loans which have financed over eight thousand houses, and increasingly encouraged local companies to go into the business of importing and stocking the supplies needed for both the oil facilities and the self-sustaining communities that were necessary to man the industry.

The provision of services for the growing cadre of Saudis employed by Aramco moved the company further into the sphere of encouraging other businesses. The Arab Industrial Development Department of Aramco resulted, with the company providing financial or technical assistance to local enterprises that do everything from growing vegetables for local markets, to making the bags they are carried in, to trucking produce and supplies from source to customer, to running bus companies, printing presses, electric companies, construction companies, water drilling companies, dairies, cement plants, hatcheries, and so on.

Much of the early drainage and irrigation work in the Al Hasa and Qatif Oases and in the Haradh Settlement Project was done with Aramco help and encouragement. Aramco medical services provide free care for all employees and fifty-five thousand dependents as well as serving as the foundation for the extensive government health services that are now available in the Eastern Province.

Aramco brought television to Saudi Arabia with its own station, which broadcast for several years before a national network was introduced. The oil company has for years published periodicals that not only inform readers about the company's activities but also offer local writers a forum for discussion of Islamic and Arab heritage, poetry, and literature.

Exploration by Aramco crews continues, both onshore and in the Gulf, where Hovercraft are now used to navigate the shallow coastal waters. A complete new oil-shipping terminal was put into operation in 1974, one of the largest construction projects ever undertaken by Aramco. New and expanding enterprises are continuously being built—water injection facilities, gas oil separation plants, electrostatic desalters, natural gas liquids production units, flash evaporation desalination units, asphalt plants. Aramco's work force in Saudi Arabia has reached 19,000, of whom only 1,600 are Americans.

The unfolding of the revolution caused by petroleum is not identical from country to country, of course. Its impact in Saudi Arabia, for example, is very much affected by the size of the country and the fact that its population is dispersed over a wide area. Tiny Kuwayt has few natural resources besides petroleum and natural gas, and a population of only 925,000, most of which is attracted by the oil industry so that it is concentrated in the capital city. Massive oil revenues have made it possible to provide all the social services and income that Kuwaytis can absorb and still pay foreigners to operate Kuwayt's oil industry and other activities. The local market is too small to justify large-scale diversification, so that the Kuwaytis are in the unusual position of being occupied largely in spending and investing money. Abu Dhabi faces much the same problem in the future, but her oil development is much more recent and plans for utilizing it are in the process of being worked out.

Bahrayn, with only small limited oil resources, has been forced to follow a much more frugal road in planning the maximum advantages that can be realized from her resources and to seek other activities, like aluminum manufacture, that can broaden her economic base and provide further income to finance the social services that Bahraynis desire. Oman also appears to have a limited amount of oil, but is just now starting along the road which Bahrayn embarked on right after World War II, so that Oman should be able to profit from her neighbor's experience in making the wisest choices for spending her income.

The transformation of formerly barren desert areas into bustling industrial complexes, crisscrossed by highways, pipelines, and utility grids, and dotted with modern towns and ports, is not the only legacy of the oil industry. In all the Arab countries, underground oil is the property of the state. The royalties paid by oil companies for exploration rights and profits from sales of crude oil that accrue to the local government provide the revenue to transform the rest of the country. In all of the countries of the Arabian Peninsula, whether they have any known oil reserves or not, the petroleum industry is one of the principal sources of revenue because dozens of oil companies are competing in searching for new fields, and they pay fees and bonuses to the host government in return for concessions to explore for oil.

Once oil in commercial quantities is found, the usual practice of oil companies until comparatively recently was to allocate a fixed percentage of their revenues as payment to the local state treasury. In countries where one family controlled all political power, as is the usual case in the Arabian Peninsula, a share of the revenues due to the local government—perhaps a quarter or a third of the total—went directly to the ruling monarch.

Some of these countries have only recently set up state trea-

Abu Dhabi town in 1949, before petroleum and independence.

suries and begun operating under organized administrations. The early oil concession agreements in Kuwayt, Bahrayn, Saudi Arabia, and Qatar have all been revised to give the local government a much larger share in the profits. The precedent for a fifty-fifty split was established in 1950 by Aramco, and

Modern Abu Dhabi from the air.

other countries soon sought the same terms. New concessions offshore in Saudi Arabia and Kuwayt embodied this arrangement and provided leverage for forcing the revision of old concessions.

Then in 1960 five oil-producing countries formed the Organization of Petroleum Exporting Countries (OPEC) and succeeded in freezing the posted prices of crude oil so that their share remained stable rather than fluctuating with changing market conditions. OPEC began demanding that oil companies operating within members' borders treat the host governments as full partners in the industry. Saudi Arabia negotiated an agreement to take over 25 percent ownership of Aramco producing facilities and in 1974 upped its share to 60 percent. In ensuing negotiations the Saudi Arabian government sought complete control, with a contract arrangement for the foreign companies which became partners to continue certain activities such as refining and marketing on a concession basis. Qatar has taken over 60 percent control of its oil production industry, and Kuwayt took over complete control of the Kuwayt Oil Company in 1975.

Several governments of Middle Eastern countries have set up their own national oil companies, such as the Kuwayt National Oil Company, or special agencies to participate in the industry, such as the General Organization of Petroleum and Minerals (Petromin) in Saudi Arabia. The existence of these local institutions permits different kinds of concessionary arrangements from those negotiated in the 1930s. Instead of leaving all the technical activities up to the oil company in return for a fixed percentage fee, local governments now make agreements for joint exploration, production, refining, and marketing, with contracts stipulating that substantial capital investments will be made by the foreign company, either as a bonus payment to the local government or in the form of large exploration outlays. All or part of these initial expenses can be recovered by the foreign company if commercial production of oil is realized.

Governments seek to reduce their dependence on petroleum by developing a whole range of industries related to oil, integrating all these activities into a national economic development plan which will diversify the country's economic base. National oil companies or government agencies in Saudi Arabia, Kuwayt, and Iran have entered into agreements with foreign firms for the joint production of one or more of a wide range of petrochemicals, such as ammonia, urea, and plastics.

These are sweeping changes within the oil-producing countries themselves, but it has been the success of the Organization of Petroleum Exporting Countries in controlling the price of crude oil that has rocked the rest of the world. Formed in Baghdad in 1960 by Iran, Venezuela, Saudi Arabia, Kuwayt, and Iraq, OPEC today includes Algeria, Ecuador, Gabon, Indonesia, Libya, Nigeria, Qatar, and the United Arab Amirates.

In the beginning the Western world did not take seriously the oil-producing states' desire for a larger share of the income from their oil revenues and for greater control over their development. However, events in the years 1971–74 brought a complete turnaround in the Near East oil picture. Libya succeeded in negotiating a substantial raise in prices and taxes paid by Occidental Petroleum Company at a moment in time when the Suez Canal was closed. Tapline had been shut down by a bulldozer accident, and western Europe suddenly found itself short of oil. Libya's success pointed the way for OPEC to negotiate the Tehran Agreement of 1971, which started the steep rise in the price of oil. In 1972 the oil countries demanded participation in companies operating within their borders, starting at one-quarter equity, and rising gradually in steps to 51 percent participation by 1982. In 1973

Iran took over all the oil installations in that country, guaranteeing in return a twenty-year supply of oil to the foreign companies which had been operating there. Iraq and Algeria soon followed suit, and Libya nationalized specific companies.

By 1973 OPEC controlled 85 percent of the world's oil exports, and this extraordinary situation coincided with a steadily increasing demand for greater and greater amounts of energy around the world. When demand exceeds supply, the seller can set the price. OPEC did exactly that late in 1973 by quadrupling the price which its members expected to receive. The shock effect of this action might have been more effectively resisted by the oil importers had it not coincided with the 1973 Arab oil embargo against the countries which helped Israel in fighting Egypt in the Sinai Peninsula and Syria on the Golan Heights.

That embargo was actually imposed by the Organization of Arab Exporting Countries, a smaller group than OPEC, which was established in 1967 on the initiative of Saudi Arabia, and included Kuwayt, Algeria, Bahrayn, Iraq, Libya, and the United Arab Amirates. The cutoff of Arab oil forced the industrialized nations to face three stark facts: Their economies were so dependent on petroleum that they were forced to pay whatever price the oil exporting states agreed on; the non-Arab oil-producing nations could not supply their needs, so that a long-term embargo could prove disastrous to economies of some countries, particularly Japan; and finally, the Arab oil embargo had coincided by accident with almost the exact moment in history when production of oil in the United States began to decline. Although the United States was not hit as hard by the embargo as Europe and Japan, she was no longer the world's leading oil producer. Saudi Arabian production almost equaled American in 1974, and Soviet oil production moved into first place in 1975.

It is important to realize that these events do not have a cause and effect relationship. The increasing energy shortages in industrialized countries, which result from continuous multiple rises in demand, were inevitable, with or without OPEC or the Arab oil embargo. OPEC members successfully raised oil prices because of the continually mounting demand for energy, and the oil embargo forced the industrial countries to face their dilemma of increasing dependence on foreign oil to meet energy demands. Nor is there anything illegal about an oil embargo. Every country in the world is privileged to decide to whom it wishes to sell its products. The regulatory aspects of OPEC bother some critics because the organization is fixing prices, but non-member producers like Canada have followed OPEC in raising prices. The sensible way to combat high prices is to decrease demand so that the seller lowers his price. Energy conservation and the search for alternate sources of energy are necessary both to lower costs and to protect an exhaustible resource.

The sudden large increase in oil prices has caused a major shift in world monetary reserves. OPEC revenues in 1974 were so large that the oil-producing countries took in $60 billion more than they could spend. Although there was considerable fear among world economists that surplus oil money from the Middle East would swamp the international monetary system, the surplus cash was easily absorbed by existing banks and lending institutions.

The OPEC countries have used much of their increased revenue for the import of goods and services from the developed world. In 1975 world oil production leveled off as the industrial nations reduced their petroleum imports. This cut surplus OPEC revenues in half. On their part, OPEC monetary authorities have followed a responsible and constructive course to avoid actions that would unsettle international financial markets.

The Arab leaders know full well that their oil wealth is a potent weapon, which has put them in a position where they can finally bargain from strength, but they also recognize that employing such a weapon destructively could shatter the world economy and with it the markets for their only resource.

If great wealth endows the oil rulers with staggering responsibilities for promoting international fiscal stability, it also requires the leaders of the industrial countries to seek their active participation. Saudi Arabia in 1974 possessed the second largest monetary reserves in the world, with West Germany in first place and the United States in third. Wealth begets power in modern society, and the oil producers are going to exercise the power that their wealth implies. They should be encouraged to exercise it wisely.

Unfortunately, Western reaction to this extraordinary change in circumstances has been that it is grossly unfair. Yet the price of petroleum, like the price of wheat, is determined by demand in world markets. The energy crisis is a matter of cost as well as of availability. Furthermore, our own self-interest may blind us to what is the best course for the Arab governments. Arab constraints on level of production may be legitimate conservation measures, and producers may prefer to stretch out production to fit their local capital needs, keeping prices very high, rather than pump more oil than the local economy demands in order to meet foreign needs. In making such assessments, petroleum ministers like Shaykh Yamani of

Offshore plant enables the Dubay Petroleum Company to produce, store, and export crude oil with no dependence on shore-based facilities. The square building is living quarters for plant personnel.

Saudi Arabia are following sound economic principles learned at Western universities.

Since OPEC's successful hiking of oil prices, Saudi Arabia (with Kuwayt and Qatar following her lead) has become a potent factor in any attempt to balance power in the Middle East. This represents no change in Arab policy, but rather a change in Arab ability to influence the course of events. The wealthy countries of the Arabian Peninsula will use their resources to push their political interests, as nations do all over the world, and their interests include a fair settlement for the Palestinians. Saudi Arabia and Kuwayt have chosen to follow a moderate policy, which seeks to maintain friendship both with the West and with all their Arab neighbors. Their stand is constantly challenged by extreme pro-Arab, anti-Western radicals throughout the Arab world. The latter are dedicated to the complete destruction of the State of Israel, which they regard as a creation of the West, and they are armed by Iron Curtain countries via Iraq and Syria. The civil war which these radical elements provoked in Lebanon in 1975 should indicate the futility of revolutionary solutions to the Palestinian problem and suggest the wisdom of negotiations with moderate Arab leaders as a more equitable alternative.

The focus of the debate between the oil producers and the oil consumers has been shifted to the United Nations. The whole bloc of developing countries would like to have more equitable arrangements worked out for arriving not only at oil prices, but also at fair prices for other raw materials and commodities that are exported and for manufactured goods and machinery which they import from industrialized nations. Rising prices of energy, rising prices of food (including North American food grains), high costs of industrial goods, growing scarcities of raw materials, world inflation, and the continuous fluctuation in the value of currencies are making it increasingly evident that all the peoples on our small earth are interdependent and must work together to meet our interlocking needs.

10

Development

The oil-producing countries of the Arabian Peninsula face a set of problems which are unique in the history of mankind. Never before have governments set out to provide a comfortable and dignified standard of living for every citizen in the land, possessing far more than adequate financial resources to accomplish the task. There are no guidelines to follow, and the Arab nations must decide how to chart a course that will lead to the desired goal, avoiding the pitfalls of greed, materialism, and decadence that generally result from having too much money.

Sharing is an ancient Arab tradition, so that the distribution of rapidly increasing oil wealth among the countries of the Arabian Peninsula is well under way. Kuwayt began the practice in the early 1950s, with Saudi Arabia and Abu Dhabi following suit as their revenues increased beyond their own immediate needs. The quadrupled oil incomes since 1973 have spawned huge capital reserves which countries with small populations can share with less privileged neighbors without experiencing any hardship at home.

Petroleum is, unfortunately, not an inexhaustible resource. If the industrialized nations continue to burn energy at present rates of consumption, within about fifty years the bulk of the proven oil reserves in the Middle East will have been tapped and production will start to decline. New reserves are being discovered, but the fact remains that world energy demands are increasing in exponential multiples, and the period in which petroleum can meet those needs falls within the lifetime of children born this year. Demand patterns will also change as alternate sources of energy are sought and developed. The way in which the oil-producing countries spend their income right now will determine the kind of life faced by the next generation.

However, money and the things it can buy are only part of the ingredients essential to modernization. The traveler in the desert, though he be carrying a sack of gold, can die of hunger or thirst if he does not know how to find food or water. At the moment petroleum income beyond the Arabs' wildest dreams is providing the funds to buy everything under the sun, and if oil was an inexhaustible resource and world demand for energy continued strong indefinitely, then the Arabs could all retire to a life of ease in air-conditioned villas, paying foreigners to do all the work involved in extracting and refining petroleum and providing the good life for its fortunate possessors.

The dramatic remolding of a whole way of life in a region as harsh and hostile as the Arabian Peninsula is no easy undertaking. The availability of unlimited capital does not change the fact that resources other than petroleum are very scarce, that huge areas are arid from lack of water, and that fresh water is a very expensive commodity to produce and transport—so expensive that a Saudi prince charged with tackling water problems can examine seriously the possibility of towing icebergs from the Antarctic as a source of fresh water and a means of causing artificial precipitation over the Arabian Peninsula.

Because the time-frame in which the Arabs must work is greatly telescoped, wise investments in the next fifteen or twenty years must set the stage for further growth. Foolish decisions now can lead to disaster later on.

No decisions will be so crucial as those which determine the development of human resources, for after the oil is gone, people will remain. If Arab leaders tried to describe the situation in which they would like to find their people when that time comes, presumably they would aspire to a comfortable living standard that could be sustained—without oil. How can that goal be reached? How can human resources be developed to the point where they can maintain economic growth? What are the programs that must be instituted now to assure that eventuality? Experimental agriculture to find new ways of cultivating desert lands? Long-range programs in hydrography to develop sources of water, and to train the necessary researchers and technicians? Massive vocational programs to provide technical workers for small industries which can diversify economies and relieve dependence on imported goods? Sophisticated research to perfect new sources of energy (where better than the Arabian desert to study solar power?) and other substitutes for the resources on which industrial society now depends? Crash courses in finance and investment management so that petrodollars invested in industrial countries will provide continuing income apart from oil production? Concentration on philosophy, theology, and ethics in order to build moral fiber independent of worldly goods? Lots of attention to art, architecture, landscaping, music, drama, literature, poetry, and other aspects of high culture to shape a good life based on sensual experience, while the state takes care of social welfare?

These are not simple choices, for no one knows where any of them will lead. A quarter century of attempted modernization of impoverished countries in other parts of the world through external development aid programs has had varied and sometimes very dubious results, and has taught a negative lesson—that industrialization is no magic solution—rather than providing any positive formula. Even the industrialized nations are gradually realizing, to their sorrow, that affluence does not guarantee either individual satisfaction or social stability.

Even if the Arab countries can correctly make the momentous decisions facing them, there is tremendous built-in resistance to basic structural change within the society of the Arabian Peninsula. The poor climate for agriculture and scanty natural resources have never supported more than a thin and scattered population. Consequently the countries there are dependent not only on imported manufactured goods, but on imported food and agricultural raw materials as well. Markets are so narrow that the potential for economic diversification is limited, and the development costs of administration, of infrastructure like roads and ports, and of social services like health clinics and school systems are very high when spread over such a large area.

However, transportation and communications facilities are one of the first requirements of the petroleum industry, so that roads, airports, ports, and telecommunications are undertaken immediately when oil in commercial quantities is discovered. Manpower skills necessitate training programs and schools. The oil countries of the Arabian Peninsula have un-

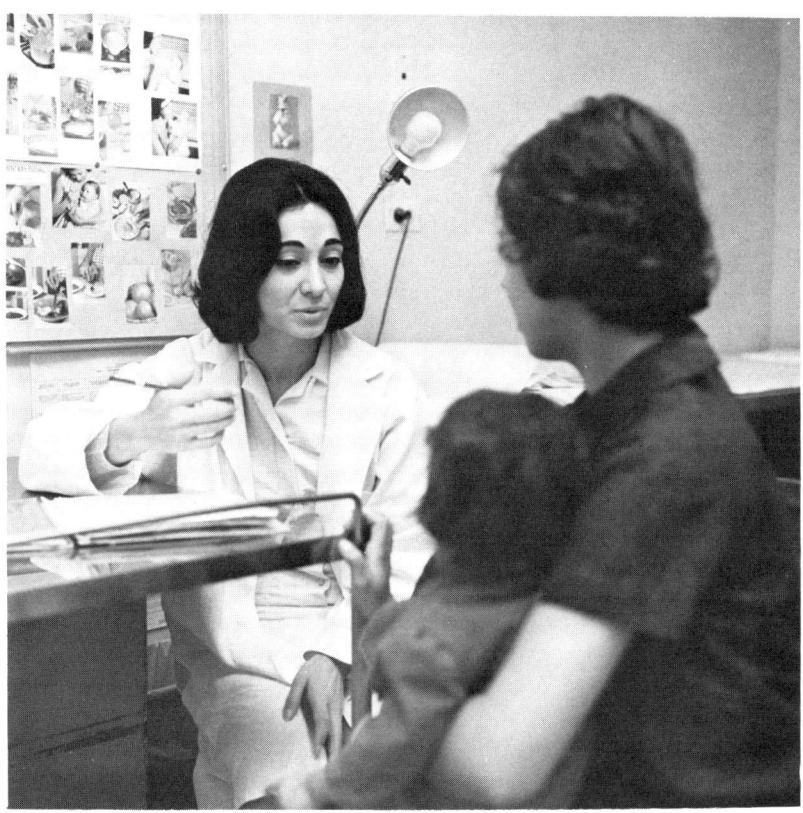

An Aramco doctor examines an employee's child at the Dhahran Health Center.

usually modern facilities for their populations and stage of economic development. Once such facilities are constructed, the local people acquire both a new kind of mobility and a whole range of new activities, including contacts with the outside world—contacts that have profound social effects. In much of Yemen and the shaykhdoms without petroleum, the old tribal organization of society still prevails, but in Kuwayt, Bahrayn, and Qatar the outward trappings of tradition have largely disappeared. Saudi Arabia, Abu Dhabi, and Dubay are well into the transition process. The fisherman, the oasis farmer, and the nomadic herdsman are gradually leaving their subsistence way of life and being drawn into wage-earning jobs. Government programs in education, health, and housing are rapidly modifying tribal customs and changing traditional outlooks. Acceptance of one's fate is giving way to rising expectations for a better life.

Although capital is available, the countries of the Arabian Peninsula lack many of the other essentials for modernization—skills, institutions, and organizational structures. The labor force is small and comparatively unskilled. It is easier to divert money into consumption, construction, and services as Kuwayt has done, than to develop institutions and new economic activities. Resistance to change is strong in that part of society that is still traditional and tribal. Formal education and welfare systems are in the process of being established, but manpower determines the speed with which facilities can be provided. Education is free and compulsory to age sixteen in Kuwayt, Bahrayn, and Qatar, free but not compulsory in Saudi Arabia because the needed schools are still being built and the needed teachers still being recruited abroad. The state provides these social services, which minimizes community initiative in supporting them.

Modern technical skills are still very much concentrated in the oil and construction industries, with the rest of the population having only a limited involvement in modern technologies. Yet provision by government of welfare services diminishes the attractiveness of blue collar occupations, and these are more often than not filled by workers from other coun-

Government employees attending class at the Public Administration Institute in Riyadh, capital of Saudi Arabia.

tries. A minuscule middle class is just in the process of being formed by successful merchants, construction and transport company entrepreneurs, civil servants, and professionals educated abroad, but many of these are expatriate Arabs from neighboring countries rather than local citizens.

Governing structures are in the process of change from private shaykhdoms to public administrations and treasuries, which require a breathing space to sort out priorities and solidify their operations. Codification of modern civil law is under way, but the rules of the game may be novel or ambiguous in the interim. Contact with the outside world and involvement in worldwide economic systems are rapidly increasing, but the impact is confusing and unsettling to those still thinking in traditional ways.

The great gap between the rich and the poor, between the urban dweller and the rural farmer or herdsman in the Arabian Peninsula has been widened by burgeoning oil wealth. Abu Dhabi has one of the highest per capita incomes in the world; the People's Democratic Republic of Yemen one of the lowest. Sweeping economic changes are inevitably disruptive.

The transformation of a traditional tribal society into a modern industrial economy within a matter of decades is an incredibly complex task. Although problems vary from country to country in the Arabian Peninsula, Saudi Arabia's example is fairly typical of the difficulties which face all the Arab leaders of the region.

Saudi Arabia has enormous income from its single most important natural resource, but other resources are very limited and in an early stage of development. Nearly three-quarters of the population is still engaged in agriculture, including herding sheep, goats, and camels. Most cultivation is in the many oases and in the highlands of Asir where heavier rainfall supports terraced farming. The production of dates, which used to be a major food crop, is declining in importance. Other crops are wheat, barley, maize, millet, alfalfa, rice, and fruit and vegetables. The production of these crops is insufficient for local needs, however, and has to be supplemented by imports.

The nomadic Bedouin tend herds of camels (300,000 in all), sheep and goats (3,200,000), providing milk, meat, and wool. Thus animal husbandry forms an important source of agricultural income. The commercial fishing industry has considerable potential, but is undeveloped.

The country is in the process of building the facilities essential to modernizing its economy. The basic requirement for the development of agriculture is water supply. Ambitious oasis reclamation, water development and conservation schemes have been undertaken by the government. A large number of dams, reservoirs, and irrigation and flood drainage projects are under way in the various oases.

Saudi Arabia has other minerals in addition to oil, but they have not yet been exploited. Substantial phosphate reserves have been found near the Jordanian border, iron ore along the Red Sea coast, and heavy minerals along the Red Sea floor. There is already a small output of salt, gypsum, and limestone.

Electric power generation is limited except in the oil fields, but development is occurring in the principal cities. Power plants are fueled by natural gas or diesel oil.

Industries range from the very primitive to the very sophisticated. Besides traditional cottage industries, Saudi Arabia has many small-scale enterprises manufacturing soap, pottery, furniture, and household articles. Modern large-scale industry, while limited by the small size of the internal market and the shortage of skilled labor, includes a urea fertilizer plant in Dammam, a steel rolling mill in Jiddah, cement plants, a detergent factory, food processing plants, and building material processing. Future industrial growth is most likely in petrochemicals.

One of the most flourishing industries over the years has been the construction industry as public funds have gone into dams and irrigation projects, highways, airports, government buildings, and both public and private housing. Saudi Arabia's principal towns today look much like large construction camps.

Modernization requires transportation and communication facilities. Until 1964 the only surfaced roads were found in the Jiddah-Mecca-Medina triangle and in the oil field network. Since then road building has been given priority in development planning, and now over five thousand miles of paved roads link the main towns along the Red Sea coast to all the oases in the central region, which are in turn linked to the oil fields and oases in the Eastern Province, where northern links extend into Kuwayt and the entire length of Tapline to the Jordan border.

The only railroad is the government's 570 km. standard gauge line from Dammam to Riyadh.

Saudi Arabia's principal ports are Dammam on the Gulf, which has a seven-mile causeway to deep water, and Jiddah on the Red Sea. Both ports are being continuously enlarged, but are inadequate to handle current shipping needs.

The main international airports are at Jiddah, Riyadh, and Dhahran. These and several smaller airports are being steadily improved. The government-owned Saudia Airlines provides both internal service and regular flights to major capitals around the world.

The Saudi government has committed the kingdom's enormous oil revenues to a massive modernization of its economy and society. The First Five Year Development Plan, adopted in

1970, sought more rapid economic growth, the development of human resources, and the diversification of sources of national income to lessen dependence on oil. The Plan initially called for the expenditure of about $10 billion on development of agriculture and water resources and other essential infrastructure, industry projects, education and public health, and defense.

Progress in implementing that Plan was erratic. On the one hand, the financial resources available increased far beyond expectations as crude oil revenues (which provide over 90 percent of government's total income) rose sharply after 1970 due to expansion of oil production, to increased government equity share in the oil companies, and after 1973 to a nearly fivefold rise in crude oil export prices. During this period progress was made in improving electric power generating capacity, in expanding some industries such as cement, and in the growth of trade, transport, finance, real estate, and business services.

On the other hand, progress in expanding physical and social infrastructure fell below Plan targets. The major constraint was the extreme shortage of manpower at all levels: managerial, technical, skilled and unskilled workers. Therefore in 1975 government eased regulations for hiring foreigners. The Saudis undertook mineral surveys and industry feasibility studies and began seeking private investment for mineral and industrial projects.

In 1975 the Saudi government announced the Second Five Year Development Plan (1975–80) with the following goals:

To maintain the religious and moral values of Islam.
To assure the defense and internal security of the kingdom.
To maintain a high rate of economic growth.
To reduce economic dependence on export of crude oil.

To develop human resources by education, training, and raising standards of health.

To increase the well-being of all groups within the society.

To develop the physical infrastructure to support achievement of the above skills.

Because Saudi Arabia anticipates annual income approaching $30 billion a year, the Second Plan calls for public expenditures of about $142 billion, almost nine times the total projected in the First Plan. Of these proposed expenditures, a little over one-third of the total is budgeted for administration ($10 billion), defense ($22 billion), external aid, emergencies, food subsidies, general reserve, and the like.

Slightly less than two-thirds is earmarked for development expenditures: $26 billion is to develop economic resources such as water, agriculture, petroleum, minerals, electricity, manufacturing, construction, and similar activities. $32 billion is to go into physical facilities needed for development such as roads, ports, airports, communications, municipalities, and housing. Almost $23 billion is for human resource development—manpower, training, labor affairs, education, cultural activities, information services. $9.5 billion is allocated for social services, including health, social security, social insurance, youth welfare, services to nomads, and judicial systems.

The Second Plan calls for the development of water resources for inland urban, industrial, and agricultural uses, and of desalinated water for use in coastal areas. The major focus of agricultural development will be regional projects involving research, extension services, marketing and credit, and water use for the production of cereals, livestock, and vegetables and fruits. Oil and mineral survey activity will be accelerated. Additions will be made to electric power generating capacity and transmission lines.

The Plan calls for $13 billion in heavy industrial projects to be undertaken by the state agency, Petromin. These include a giant contract which Aramco will supervise to construct natural gas gathering, treatment, and transmission facilities. The gas will be used solely for domestic consumption as feed stocks for petrochemicals and fertilizer, and as fuel for industry, power generation, and desalination.

A Saudi technician in the control room at the Ras Tanura refinery in Saudi Arabia.

Two new industrial areas will be created. In Jubayl on the Gulf three ethylene-based petrochemical plants, two oil refineries, a direct reduction steel mill, and an aluminum smelter will be constructed. Nearby in Dammam three fertilizer plants will be built. Connected to Jubayl by a new trans-Peninsula pipeline, Yanbo, on the Red Sea, will be the site of another oil refinery and a petrochemical complex as well as cement, car, and tire factories.

In the field of human resource development the Plan concentrates on measures to relieve the country's extremely tight labor situation. A massive effort will be made to expand vocational training centers, largely for workers in the construction and metal-working trades. Formal education facilities will be expanded at elementary, intermediate, secondary, and university levels, with more programs in teacher and technical training at the high school level and in professional-level training for medicine and engineering.

Even so, the country's rate of manpower development will fall further behind projected manpower requirements, and there will be a need for five hundred thousand foreign workers.

The nation's physical infrastructure will be improved by adding eight thousand miles of main, secondary, and paved feeder roads, by enlarging the ports of Jiddah and Dammam, and by upgrading airport facilities. The seven major cities will be linked by a telecommunications network that should eventually provide 90 percent of the population with long distance service. All the major cities will undergo master development plans, and an additional 358,000 housing units will be provided.

Overall, the expenditures for the actual construction of all these facilities over the five-year period will be $73 billion, or half the Plan total.

Implementation of this dramatic Plan will place considerable strain on the Saudi government, which must overcome three major bottlenecks. The most serious stricture is inadequate port capacity and cargo handling ability, which already causes a three-to-five-month delay in unloading arriving ships. The second crucial bottleneck—manpower—has already been mentioned. The third major problem is insufficient local institutions to finance industrial and other projects.

Hence outside business corporations and governmental agencies will continue to play a major role in Saudi Arabia's development. Foreign enterprise will provide capital equipment, undertake construction and management contracts, and participate in joint ventures in public and private projects. The government has actively sought the cooperation of international and bilateral aid agencies for development assistance, and investment guarantee and technical cooperation agreements have been signed with a number of non-Communist countries. The United States/Saudi Arabia Joint Economic Commission, established in 1975, provides a framework for extensive American technical assistance in a variety of projects.

Thus continued foreign involvement, with Americans particularly welcome, will be part of Saudi Arabia's transformation into a modern society.

Other oil-producing states in the Peninsula are undertaking similar measures for modernization, although on a smaller scale than Saudi Arabia.

11

Values

The test of success in the Arabian Peninsula will not be how fast the several countries modernize or adopt Western attitudes and institutions, but rather how well they nurture and develop their own potential for making their unique cultural contribution. The Arabs remember with pride the glory of the Moslem Empire in the eighth, ninth, and tenth centuries, when Arab learning and culture dominated the Mediterranean world, and they dream of another flowering of Arab genius. Poverty and backwardness have been their lot for centuries, but today oil prosperity makes almost anything possible. Now the Arabs speak of *nahda,* which means "rebirth." If an Arab renaissance does materialize, it may well result from an amalgamation of Western technology and Arab values, in much the same way that a fusion of cultures provided dynamism for that glorious Moslem Empire. The challenge is, of course, for the Arabs to select the best of both worlds and make it their own.

People everywhere in the world strive for accomplishments in which they can take pride. In many parts of the world these efforts are not directed toward the acquisition of material possessions, but rather toward the attainment of intangible rewards such as titles, intellectual discoveries, or a reputation for wisdom or bravery. In the Arabian Peninsula the Bedouin put great store in those achievements which were appropriate to their stark desert environment—honor, hospitality, skill in organizing and in raiding, and mobility in fighting. These ancient nomadic virtues have been supplemented over the centuries by the ethical values of Islam, which encourage brotherhood and a deep veneration of religious law to guide social conduct. The strict observance of Moslem law has been much modified in the countries of the Fertile Crescent and North Africa by colonial rule and a persistent intrusion of outside ideas, but the people of the Arabian Peninsula, because of their very poverty and remoteness, have maintained their personal philosophy with very little outside interference.

If we judge the governments of the Arabian Peninsula on the basis of their own particular situations, we have to admit that they are coping remarkably well and are maintaining considerable stability in a period of great flux. No government on the Peninsula has yet existed for half a century, and some of them have less than a decade of experience to draw on. Yet they are plunging into the modern world with courage and enthusiasm and considerable flair. Their governing institutions are not carbon copies of any found elsewhere, but are unique.

We may wonder how long paternalistic rule by traditional tribal chiefs can endure or how well it can adapt and adjust to changing conditions, but more radical leadership would probably be much less stable. Along with their unique mechanisms for national rule the Arab leaders have strengthened legal and security arrangements that minimize crime and disorder. Moslem law is very strict in its doctrines and severe in its punishments, and its prompt application effectively discourages thievery, begging, personal assault, and the other ills that are bred by urban society. Local police and army, recruited from the population at large, are able to cope with the ordinary needs for internal security. When unusual situations or public disorders arise, the Arab kings and shaykhs turn to their personal security forces. The king's army in Saudi Arabia, for example, is an elite National Guard, recruited from among the noble tribes of the country, paid by the monarch, and kept relatively isolated from the general public. Its loyalties are the traditional desert loyalties of the Bedouin to their shaykh, an effective instrument in this demanding environment.

Even the great changes which have taken place in the last twenty-five years as the result of a startling infusion of oil wealth have occurred in too short a time to effect fundamental adjustments away from the Bedouin ethos and the traditional values of Islam. Religion is a very constant presence in daily life, visible not only in the regular prayer ritual which the Arabs perform without self-consciousness, but in multiple tiny reminders that punctuate every activity. God's blessing is invoked in connection with almost any undertaking, however small, and the Arabs constantly remind each other that God knows man's destiny so that he must rely on God in every situation. Even the airplane stewardess adds to her announcement of an imminent arrival, "We will land in a few minutes, God willing." The Peninsula Arabs have never faced the choice of rejecting their Islamic heritage in favor of an alien philosophy, and consequently step into the modern era without any confusion as to their own identity.

Confusion, when it arises, is apt to come with the staggering number of foreigners being attracted to the Arabian Peninsula by investment and job opportunities. There is no way that

Kuwayt can have three-quarters of its labor force foreign, Qatar and the United Arab Amirates have half their population alien, Bahrayn a fifth, without the mixed composition of the labor force having an enormous social impact on the citizens of those countries. Saudi Arabia cannot bring over half a million foreigners into a country of 5 million people without having an impact that neither the Saudis nor the countries that will furnish the technicians can yet predict. The Saudis have always preferred American technology when they could get it, but will they perhaps decide to slow down their headlong plunge into the modern world if they find their traditional way of life being swamped by an overwhelming influx of Westerners?

There will certainly be conflicts between those planners whose primary concern is economic growth and more conservative Arabs who prefer to avoid inundation by foreigners in order to preserve the character of Arab society. Ordinarily the government of a developing country could not choose to delay economic development in order to guard cultural homogeneity because of the pressures of rising popular expectations, but the situation in the Arabian Peninsula is unique in that development planners in oil countries are anticipating wants and providing social services and improving public welfare faster than public demand for them has crystallized.

Pressures will come, not from an impoverished peasantry, because the poor are being provided with opportunities for economic betterment almost faster than they can adjust to them, but rather from those elements of Peninsula society which are well enough educated to understand the adjustments they face. These include both indigenous citizens, who feel a need for greater participation in the political process, and a very large element of foreign Arabs working in the

Peninsula—well-paid and living very comfortably, but not always popular with the native-born, who resent them because they feel threatened by their numbers and expertise.

There are also large numbers of unskilled laborers—from Yemen, Oman, Iran, Pakistan, and India—who are hired to do the menial and distasteful jobs, and are more used to disciplined work habits than the locals. Yemenis have migrated in such numbers as to cause a severe manpower shortage in Southern Yemen and now must pay a large fee before leaving that insures their return. These foreigners are paid as little as possible and live miserably in shantytowns around all the major cities. They are a silent blot on the landscape, afraid to express any dissatisfaction for fear of being deported, yet they are essential to economic growth, just as are their countrymen in the white-collar and technician ranks. There are also highly skilled Arab professionals from Egypt, Lebanon, Palestine, and Iraq who have been filling top advisory posts as fledgling governments set up machinery to deal with the influx of capital and technology, but they too see local aspirants seeking education abroad in ever-increasing numbers and recognize that in a few years they will be replaced and have no place to go. All three of these categories put added strain on infant public services, particularly housing, which is becoming impossibly expensive in many cities. Without avenues open to acquiring citizenship, none of them feels economically or politically secure.

The Jahra Gate in the old city wall of Kuwayt frames modern buildings within.

The modernization that oil revenue makes possible includes, indeed requires, education, and thus opens the door to foreign political ideas, which are an impetus for change and dissatisfaction. Travel abroad and the rapid spread of television have a major impact in spreading new attitudes. Where a middle class of bureaucrats, teachers, and students develops, as it did in Bahrayn earlier than in the rest of the Arabian Peninsula, pressures build up for political reform.

Elsewhere the educated young are bound to be in the forefront of reform movements and political causes such as solidarity against Israel. The potential for frustration will greatly increase if local economies have difficulty in absorbing professional skills that result from too many students choosing elite careers in law or literature and too few choosing engineering or agronomy. This has already begun to happen in Bahrayn and Qatar, and to a lesser extent in Sharjah.

Suspicion of foreign ideas is much stronger in the more isolated regions of the Peninsula than in the oil towns. In the highlands of Oman and Yemen and the remote Hadramaut Valley society is still tribalized and political loyalties are to local and sectarian interests. The chiefs are more a law unto themselves, with government control very limited. Honor and revenge are still uppermost in personal relations, and blood feuds still operate. Courage is highly valued and every man wears his weapon in his belt. Here resistance to outside ideas and influences is very strong. However, to balance this determined individualism of the mountain tribes there is a unifying sense of common identity based on a shared ethical code and proud historical traditions. Although religious and tribal differences cause local frictions, there are no irreconcilable ethnic, cultural, or religious differences in the Arabian Pen-

A former pearl diver of Bahrayn uses his knowledge of the sea and ships to produce scale models of traditional sailing craft.

insula. Petty quarrels arise more over who should be running things than over how they should be run.

Patterns of living and thinking in rural areas still reflect the conviction that forces beyond the control of man are guiding his existence, but the towns of the Arabian Peninsula have all the excitement of a new frontier. The streets bustle with vehicles of every description, and heavy machinery of one kind or another seems constantly standing by to demolish the inadequate and make room for the new. Urban landscapes are a startling mélange of skyscrapers, broad boulevards, modern villas, and the quaint wooden shuttered and balconied facades of an earlier era. Probably the most conspicuous characteristic of cities today is the empty lots, littered with rubble and stacks of building materials, which are to be transformed tomorrow or next month into jewels of Moorish or modern architecture.

There is more to the excitement than construction and a vast array of imported goods, however. There is also an atmosphere of things happening, of everyone being busy and involved. There are no weary-looking apathetic bodies sitting or lying on sidewalks or under trees with apparently nothing to do, no place to go, and nothing to keep body and soul together, as is so common in many developing countries of the tropical world. One sees few beggars, for plenty of jobs are available and begging is against the law. Police pick up people begging and take them to institutions to learn a skill and be put to work.

Because populations are not large, oil wealth is adequate to provide opportunity for all the people of the Arabian Peninsula. The problem is not funds, but the provision of the facilities which the funds make possible and the skills to run them. The Arabs today are absorbed in that Herculean task, but the pace of life has not become frantic. The Arabs retain their instinctive serenity and their ability to make every visitor feel not only welcome, but as though his call is the most important thing in the world and gives his welcoming host as much pleasure as it does the guest. The courtly Arab manners have not changed, but Arab talents are now engaged in planning and building on a scale that is changing the Arabian Peninsula beyond belief. Decision-making has become the way of life for the officials of government and business, and the rest of the population is being pressed into the execution of those decisions.

May Allah grant them the wisdom to choose well and the courage to guard the values that give their way of life pride and dignity.

Index

Abbasid, 53, 55, 56, 62
Abdul Aziz ibn Saud (King), 62, 72, 97, 100, 101, 103, 141
Abraham, 30, 44, 45, 67
Abu Bakr, 46, 48, 50
Abu Dhabi, 14, 26, 76, 108, 110, 111, 119, 134, 151, 155, 161, 166, 168
Aden, 11, 12, 18, 61, 94, 99, 100, 111, 112, 114, 135
Africa, 26, 30, 36, 41, 42, 55, 56, 59, 68, 70, 72, 134, 135, 140
Agriculture. *See* Farming
Ajman, 14, 108
Alexandria 49, 50
Al Buraymi Oasis, 108, 121
Al Hasa Oasis, 20, 149
Al Khalifa family, 60, 106, 120, 124
Al Kharj, 21, 145
Al Sabah family, 60, 105
Al Saud family, 60, 76, 97, 100-102, 120
Al Thani family, 107
Ali, 43, 50, 52
Allah, 42, 64, 65
Amir, 60, 84, 85
Anayzah tribe, 103, 120
Arab League, 125-127, 135
Arab unity, 124-130
Arabian American Oil Company (Aramco), 95, 141-150, 152, 173
Arabian Gulf, 18, 25, 26, 30, 36-38, 42, 57, 59, 60, 62, 70, 85, 99, 100, 105-107, 111, 124, 130-136, 141, 150, 170, 174
Arabian Nights, 17
Arabic, 28, 30, 31, 36, 55, 56, 64, 67, 71-78, 125, 148
Archeology, 38, 39, 42, 139
Asir Province, 20, 37, 121, 168

Baghdad, 17, 53, 56, 104, 155
Bahrayn (Bahrein), 13, 26, 30, 38, 60, 61, 76, 94, 105-107, 116, 119-124, 130, 131, 135, 141-145, 150-152, 166, 179, 182
Bedouin, 22, 23, 28, 30, 33-36, 46, 59, 62, 78, 79, 82, 101, 104, 108, 110, 117, 121, 169, 177, 178
Berbers, 53
Britain. *See* Great Britain
Byzantium, 48, 49, 53

Caliph, 17, 35, 46, 48-56
Camel, 22, 25, 31, 32, 35, 39, 76, 168, 169
Caravan, 18, 30, 41, 45, 56
Christianity, 42-46, 65, 67, 129
Cities, 37, 41-44, 81, 82, 90-92, 114, 119, 129, 169, 174
Civil law, 25, 101, 168
Climate, 18-27, 93, 164
Clothing, 92-94

Communism, 70, 114, 115, 137
Constantinople, 49, 56
Constitutions, 100, 106, 107, 109, 112, 116
Construction, 12, 13, 90-92, 105, 143, 148, 149, 170, 172, 184

Damascus, 49, 52, 53, 56
Dammam, 143, 145, 148, 169, 170, 174
Dates, 25, 32, 33, 59, 74, 168
Defense, 129, 137, 171, 172
Desert, 18-28, 31-35, 41, 49, 55, 79, 82, 105, 108, 144, 146, 151, 162, 163
Development planning, 161-175
Dhahran, 143-145, 149, 170
Dhofar Province, 39, 99, 114, 122, 124, 133
Diriyah, 62, 100
Divorce, 88-90
Dubay (Dubai), 14, 26, 88, 108, 110, 119, 124, 166

Eastern Province, 20, 26, 149, 170
Education, 61, 84, 85, 90-108, 114, 117, 121, 122, 129, 130, 148, 149, 163-167, 171, 172, 174, 179, 182
Egypt, 17, 28, 30, 48-50, 53, 56, 99, 121, 125-130, 156, 181
Egyptians, 37, 40, 62, 112
Empty Quarter, 22, 23, 108, 120, 122, 146
England, 98
English, 57, 74-76, 148
Ethiopia, 42, 135
Euphrates River, 18, 38, 49, 130
Exports, 11, 14, 156-160, 164, 169, 172, 174. *See also* Oil; Trade

Fahd (Prince), 103
Family. *See* Kinship
Farming, 11-14, 20-22, 25, 26, 31, 35, 36, 41, 42, 56, 81, 86, 101, 114, 145, 164, 166, 168-172

Fasting, 45, 65, 73
Faysal (King), 69, 99, 101, 104, 121
Fertile Crescent, 49, 177
Fertilizer, 12-14, 140, 169, 173, 174
Festivals, 72, 86
Fishing, 14, 110, 166, 169
Food, 92
Foreign workers, 92, 110, 133-136, 150, 162, 166, 167, 171, 174, 178-181
Frankincense, 39, 41, 59
French, 60, 135
Frontiers, 27, 100, 104, 111, 120, 121, 124, 131
Fujayrah, 14, 108

Golan Heights, 128, 156
Great Britain, 60, 61, 98-114, 124, 127-131, 135, 141
Great Rift Valley, 25, 26
Gulf of Aden, 18
Gulf (Arabian or Persian). *See* Arabian Gulf

Hadramaut, 61, 182
Hajj, 65
Haradh, 21, 149
Hashemite family, 50, 52, 101
Health, 84, 85, 101, 108, 148, 149, 166, 171, 172
Hebrew, 75
Hebrews, 44, 67
Hegira, 44
Hijaz, 43, 101
Himyarite kingdom, 41, 42
History, 30, 38-63, 97-115, 143-160
Honor, 33, 34, 68, 79, 93, 177, 182
Hormuz, 57, 133
Hospitality, 33, 83, 177, 184

Ibn Saud. *See* Abdul Aziz ibn Saud
Imams, 46, 57, 59, 84, 97-99, 121
Immigrants. *See* Foreign workers
Independence, 26, 97-115, 121, 125
India, 17, 30, 56-59, 181

Indian, 36, 37, 65, 77
Indian Ocean, 18, 41, 61
Indus River Valley, 38, 46, 49
Industry, 12, 13, 56, 85, 101, 139, 140, 149, 151, 155, 164, 169, 170-174. *See also* Oil
Iraq, 26, 28, 48-52, 97, 100-104, 111, 125, 126, 129-133, 137, 141, 155, 156, 181
Iran, 26, 37, 70, 111, 122, 124, 130-133, 140, 155, 156, 180
Irrigation, 21, 41, 145, 169, 170
Ishmael, 30, 44
Islam, 13, 28, 30, 34-37, 42-57, 62-72, 78, 93, 100, 104, 107, 124, 133, 137, 150, 171, 177, 178
Islamic Conference, 70
Israel, 37, 70, 99, 112, 121, 125, 127-130, 133, 137, 138, 156, 160, 182

Japan, 138, 140, 156
Jiddah, 30, 70, 75, 169, 170, 174
Jerusalem, 40, 44, 45, 49, 70, 128, 129
Jews, 37, 127-130
Jordan, 28, 37, 42, 99, 100, 104, 122, 125, 128, 129, 169, 170
Judaism, 43-46, 67, 68

Kabaah, 42, 45
Khalid (King), 22, 103, 104
Kinship, 33-35, 78-88, 110, 120, 125
Koran, 30, 43, 49, 61, 62, 67, 68, 71-74
Kuwayt (Kuweit), 13, 26, 30, 37, 38, 60, 76, 100-105, 116, 119-141, 150-156, 160, 161, 166, 170, 179

Language. *See* Arabic
Lebanon, 28, 125, 128, 147, 160, 181
Literature. *See* Poetry and literature
Livestock, 12, 13, 25, 31, 33, 35, 59, 74, 79, 83, 84, 88, 110, 141, 145, 168, 172

Madain Salah, 42
Majlis, 84, 101, 117
Marib, 41, 42
Marriage, 87, 88, 103
Mecca, 37, 42, 46, 50, 62, 65, 67, 70, 73, 101, 170
Medina, 37, 44, 48, 50, 52, 56, 62, 67, 70, 76, 101, 170
Mediterranean, 40, 41, 61, 85, 147, 176
Mesopotamia, 17, 30, 38
Minaeans, 40, 41
Minerals, 25, 30, 59, 109, 169, 171, 172
Monetary policy, 157-163, 171-175
Moslem Empire, 46-57, 72, 176
Moslem law, 12, 33-37, 62, 64, 68, 79, 84, 85, 90, 105, 107, 117, 120, 138, 177
Moslem religion. *See* Islam
Moslem World League, 70
Moslems, 36, 37, 43-57, 60-72, 87, 95-98, 117, 121, 125, 129, 130, 134
Muawiyah, 52
Muezzin, 45, 65
Muhammad (Prophet), 28, 30, 42-46, 50, 52, 61-67, 71
Muscat, 12, 30, 57, 59
Music, 72-74, 86, 164
Myrrh, 39, 41, 59

Nasser (President), 99, 126, 127
Nationalism, 106, 111-114, 125, 129, 133
National Liberation Front, 12, 112, 114, 121
Natural gas, 12, 14, 144, 146, 150, 169, 173
Nomads, 25-35, 56, 71, 79, 81-86, 90, 141, 148, 169, 172, 177
North Africa, 18, 25, 53, 68, 177

Oases, 20, 25, 30, 32, 108, 166, 168, 169, 170

INDEX

Oil, 12-14, 23-26, 31, 35-37, 74, 78, 85, 90, 101-122, 127-184
Old Testament, 34, 39, 40, 44, 139
Oman, 12, 26, 38, 57, 59, 60, 93, 97-99, 108, 114-124, 133, 135, 151, 181, 182
Organization of Petroleum Exporting Countries (OPEC), 127, 134, 154-160
Ottoman. *See* Turks

Pakistan, 38, 49, 68, 96, 133, 134, 181
Palestine, 37, 127-130, 160, 181
Palestine Liberation Organization, 130, 134
People's Democratic Republic of Yemen, 11, 26, 111-115, 131, 135, 137, 168, 181. *See also* Yemen Arab Republic
Persia, 17, 18, 32, 42, 48-57, 82, 98, 131
Persian Gulf. *See* Arabian Gulf
Petromin, 154, 173
Pilgrims, 37, 44, 45, 65, 67
Pillars of the Moslem Faith, 45, 65
Plants, 22, 23, 25, 168
Poetry and literature, 71-74, 150, 164
Political parties, 103, 105, 107, 110, 116, 118
Portuguese, 57, 59
Protectorates, 61, 111, 112, 141
Purdah, 93-96

Qatar, 13, 30, 38, 60, 61, 75, 105-108, 116, 119, 120, 124, 130, 135, 152, 154, 160, 166, 179, 182
Quraysh, 30, 43, 44, 46, 50, 52

Raiding, 34, 45, 48, 56, 62, 79, 177
Railroad, 145, 170
Rainfall, 18, 20, 22-26, 41
Ramadan, 45, 66, 67, 73, 86
Ras al Khaymah, 14, 108
Ras Tanura, 144-146, 149

Red Sea, 18, 26, 30, 42, 75, 134, 169, 170, 174
Refining. *See* Oil
Religion. *See* Islam
Riyadh, 12, 62, 96, 100, 145, 170
Romans, 40, 41
Rub al Khali. *See* Empty Quarter
Russia, 56, 57, 69. *See also* USSR

Saba, 40, 41
Sahara, 25, 55, 56, 68, 69
Sana, 11, 99
Saudi Arabia, 12, 20-22, 26, 27, 30, 60-63, 69, 75, 94, 97-104, 108, 115-137, 146-161, 166, 168-179
Saudis. *See* Saudi Arabia, Al Saud family
Semitic, 30, 72, 75
Shariah. *See* Moslem law
Sharjah, 14, 26, 76, 108, 111, 133, 182
Shaykh, 60-62, 74, 83, 84, 88, 94, 97, 100-117, 122, 124, 133, 141, 143, 165, 168, 178
Shia, 36, 52, 62, 97, 133
Shipping, 13, 30, 74, 131, 135, 140, 143-145, 148, 175
Slavery, 36, 43, 55, 68
Socialism, 112, 114, 121-124, 130, 131, 138, 160, 182
Southern Yemen. *See* People's Democratic Republic of Yemen
Soviet Union. *See* USSR
Spain, 52-54
Sports, 86
Standard Oil Company, 141
Suez Canal, 61, 111, 114, 135, 155
Sumer, 38
Sunnis, 36, 52, 60, 133, 134
Syria, 26, 28, 30, 43, 48-53, 125-130, 137, 156

Tapline, 147, 155, 170
Television, 85, 90, 149, 182
Texas Oil Company, 141
Tigris River, 18, 38, 49, 130

Tourism, 92, 114
Trade, 11, 14, 17, 38, 42, 43, 56-59, 84, 85, 92, 108, 110, 120, 122
Trade unions, 61, 105, 107, 110, 118
Tribal code, 33, 34
Tribes, 31-34, 41, 42, 46-50, 55, 56, 62, 68, 71, 83-85, 97, 101, 103, 110-112, 116, 117, 122, 165, 168, 177, 178, 182
Trucial Coast, 61, 105, 106, 108
Turkey, 56, 69, 141
Turks, 57, 60, 62, 97, 100, 125

Umar (Omar), 48-50
Umayyid, 50, 52-54
Umm al Qaywayn, 14, 108, 111
United Arab Amirates (Emirates), 14, 26, 30, 106-111, 116, 119, 121-124, 131, 135, 179
United Arab Republic. *See* Egypt
United Nations, 98, 128, 129, 134, 135
United States, 26, 114, 126, 129, 130, 135-137, 139, 140, 143, 146, 150, 156, 157, 158, 175, 179
USSR (Union of Soviet Socialist Republics), 26, 99, 114, 124-131, 136-140, 157
Uthman (Othman), 50

Wahhabis, 37, 62, 100, 101, 121, 125
Water, 11, 14, 20, 21, 25, 31-35, 40, 41, 82, 83, 90, 101, 108, 110, 121, 143, 144, 149, 162, 169-172
Welfare, 105-108, 119, 121, 163-166, 172, 179
Wildlife, 23
Women, 34, 61, 85-90, 93-96, 101, 107
World War I, 100, 127, 141
World War II, 61, 101, 125, 135, 140, 144, 151

Yemen, 11, 20, 25-30, 36, 37, 41-43, 59, 93, 97-99, 112, 116, 119, 121, 124, 127, 131, 135, 165, 181, 182
Yemen Arab Republic, 11, 41, 99, 100, 111. *See also* People's Democratic Republic of Yemen

Zaydi sect, 97, 99
Zayid (Shaykh), 108, 110
Zionism, 70, 127, 129, 134

About the Author

Mary Louise Clifford received her B.A. in Government from Cornell University and served in the United States Foreign Service before her marriage. She has lived in Lebanon and Pakistan and in five countries where her husband has been United Nations Economic Adviser—the Niger Republic, Sabah State of Malaysia, Burundi, Western Samoa, and Sierra Leone. A fact-finding trip across the Arabian Peninsula in the summer of 1975 was the high point in the preparation of this book. Her previous books include four others in the Portraits of the Nations Series (Afghanistan, Malaysia, Liberia, and Sierra Leone); a ten-volume high school textbook on the African continent; and two novels about Africa. The Cliffords live in Williamsburg, Virginia.

171429